Household Saints

ACKNOWLEDGMENTS

We would like to thank Betsy Beier and Nathaniel Marunas for their constructive input, as well as Bruce Lubin, John Dorfman, Allison Meierding, Tonia Samman, and Terry Deal for their friendship, hard work, and dedication. Thanks are also in order to Stanley Wang, Derek Lam, and Michael Willcocks for their impeccable craftsmanship. Finally, special thanks are due to Father Eugene Carrella for his wisdom and support.

Prepared by D&J Book Packaging and Media, Inc.
1361 Lexington Avenue
New York, NY 10128

Design: Laurie Dolphin and Allison Meierding
Managing Editor: Jessica Jones
Copy Editor: Terry Deal
Editorial Assistant: Tonia Samman

All images of saints are from the collection of Father Eugene Carrella.

2006 Barnes & Noble Publishing

ISBN-13: 978-0-7607-8288-0
ISBN-10: 0-7607-8288-1

Printed and bound in China
10 9 8 7 6 5 4 3 2 1

Household Saints

The HOLY FRIENDS WHO PROTECT

YOUR HOME and HEARTH

ALEXANDER JOHNSON

BARNES & NOBLE

NEW YORK

Contents

Introduction

THIS BOOK recounts the life stories of some of the remarkable religious individuals known as saints. These accounts also include descriptions of the myriad ways in which the saints can help us in our daily lives, and specifically, in this case, around the house, despite the fact that most of them lived centuries ago. But what exactly is a saint? We all use the word, but do we know what it *really* means?

A saint is a person who is formally recognized by the Catholic Church as holy and particularly close to God. They are people we can be certain are in Heaven, and as such can intercede with God for us—that is, convey our prayers to Him and put in a little added word for us. The Church believes that in order to qualify as a saint, a person must have acted as a kind of conduit for the divine power while alive on earth. In other words he or she—and saints were just as often female as male, even in such patriarchal eras as Greco-Roman antiquity and the Middle Ages—had to have performed miracles. Additionally, to be a saint, he or she would have had to have been an inspiration to those who came into contact with him or her. Saints are not only saintly themselves; they spread sanctity all around them.

As you read through this book, you'll notice that the saints each have their own departments, so to speak, known as their patronage. Being a "patron saint" can mean several things. On one hand, it can mean that the saint presides over a profession or trade, so that individuals who follow those walks of life regard him or her as their special protector and inspiration. For example, St. Martin is the patron saint of barbers and hairstylists, who may pray to him for guidance to help them cut hair better, or even to show them how to introduce spirituality into hairstyling. On the other hand, many saints are special protectors against a particular threat, which could be anything from a major calamity to a minor irritant of everyday life. We may

A saint is a person who is formally recognized by the Catholic Church as holy and particularly close to God.

pray to them to ward off a certain kind of trouble, or to comfort and strengthen us if trouble comes. For example, St. Agatha is invoked against breast cancer, St. Lawrence against kitchen accidents, and St. Anthony of Padua for help in finding lost objects.

So, how do you become a saint? Well, first of all, death is a prerequisite. To be canonized—official Church lingo for being declared a saint—you have to be in Heaven, because that is where you are needed to intercede on behalf of the rest of us down here. The process of canonization is rather complicated, and seems to have gotten more complicated with the passing centuries. It's almost like a court case, with a defense and a prosecution (sometimes known as the "devil's advocate") that try to establish whether the person in question actually performed miracles, whether the eyewitnesses were reliable—in short, whether the prospective saint was really as holy as all that. It works in stages: first you reach the stage called "servant of God," then "venerable," then "blessed" (the waiting room of sainthood), and then finally saint. Some saints made it quickly—St. Anthony of Padua took only a few months—and some very slowly. St. Martin de Porres, who died in 1639, wasn't officially recognized as a saint until 1962.

The individuals discussed in this book are not only popular patron saints beloved by Catholics the world over, they also belong to a special classification known as "household saints." Household saints are invoked for household concerns, issues that are literally close to home. Love, peace, and contentment, our personal safety and the safety of our loved ones—these are the comforts that household saints can provide, if we keep them close to our hearts. St. Valentine can help us find true love, St. Monica provides help with difficult relationships, St. Dymphna guards against anxiety,

What Exactly Are Household Saints?

There are so many saints who watch over and protect us in times of need, but few who can be classified as household saints. So, what are they and why do they exist in a class by themselves? Household saints are special because their strengths and power are directly tied to our concerns about our most prized place... our home. They also can take care of issues that are simply very personal and close to us, such as love, happiness, and good health. They can also help with the mundane parts of our lives that are less spiritual but no less important. For example, household saint St. Jude governs lost or desperate causes (whether a rebellious teenager's school attendance or rising property taxes) whereas St. Zita of Lucca is on hand to help when your vacuum cleaner gives up the ghost.

and St. Joseph can help you buy or sell a house. Believe it or not, there are even patron saints for home repair enthusiasts (St. Stephen) and people who watch television (St. Clare).

Think of the saints not as remote and forbidding spiritual giants to be approached with trepidation, but as holy friends. Reading about their lives helps us understand their spheres of influence and identify with them more closely. We come to realize that whether they lived in remotest antiquity or in the modern age, the saints started out more or less like us. They went through many of the same kinds of struggles that people do in today's world—they faced opposition from parents who didn't understand them, societies that treated them as second-class citizens, and friends who thought their spirituality was silly. They had to deal with self-doubt, and even with doubt about the existence of God.

They often lived under conditions of dire poverty and war. They had flaws—plenty of them—and had to work hard to bask in God's grace. And even though many of these life stories come down to us from documents written in ancient languages in remote times very different from our own, the human, warm personalities of the saints usually shine through.

The saints are beloved today because they are compassionate. Eternal and divine, yes, but also human and accessible. They can help us, if only we will let them.

Are the saints only for Catholics and Christians? Although they all spent their lives trying their best to spread the message of Christ and His Church, and many of them were killed for their faith, the saints are not sectarian. In life, many of them had friends and family who were not Christian. How could a saint turn down a cry for help? How could a person whose charity to others reached super-human proportions leave any human being to suffer if he or she could do something about it? In this sense, the saints are for anybody who is inspired by them and turns to them for succor or protection.

The saints are beloved today because they are compassionate. Eternal and divine, yes, but also human and accessible. They can help us, if only we will let them. Approach the saints in a spirit of humility and devotion, but also with familiarity and friendliness. Keep their likenesses close by you, let them guard and bless your home, talk to them, and most of all, listen for their guidance.

Living With Your Three Holy Friends

Included with this book are statues of three holy friends—St. Joseph, St. Jude, and St. Clare of Assisi—who perfectly embody the classification of "household saint," as they have clear dominion over certain aspects of our domestic lives. Here is what each of the holy friends in this box can do for you and how you can use their statues to help their blessings along.

St. Joseph

Thanks to his tireless search for a sheltering place for the infant Jesus to be born, St. Joseph is the patron saint of both house hunting and selling a house. If you bury a figurine of St. Joseph in your yard, it is said he will help you attract buyers and improve your chances of getting your top asking price. If you place the figurine in front of your door, the saint will bless your home. Alternately, you could display St. Joseph's likeness in a place of honor, such as the fireplace mantel, to symbolize the comforts and blessings of home and hearth.

St. Jude

St. Jude is the ever-useful and very popular patron saint of lost or desperate causes. This is commonly attributed to the fact that he was able to work so many miracles and rescue people from terrible fates. Place his figurine somewhere in your home where you have totally despaired of making any headway with the cleaning and organizing: your hopelessly cluttered study, the kitchen sink that's never empty, the bathroom that you just can't face scrubbing.

St. Clare

St. Clare is the patron saint of television because she was given the divine power to see things that were happening far away. In particular, when St. Clare was sick and confined to her cell, she saw an image of the mass being conducted in the nunnery's chapel projected on the wall. A natural place for your figurine of St. Clare is on or near your entertainment center. The saint's protective influence can help ward off bad cable reception and terrible television shows. St. Clare can even guide you in your viewing choices and inspire you and your family to choose programs that are not only entertaining, but spiritually uplifting, too.

St. Agatha

Patron Saint of

★ BREAST CANCER PATIENTS ★ FOUNDRY WORKERS ★
★ PROTECTION AGAINST FIRE ★ MOUNTAIN GUIDES ★

S]T. AGATHA was a virgin martyr of the third century A.D. She was born in Sicily to a rich and prominent family. She grew up to be a physically beautiful young woman, which attracted a great deal of attention of the wrong kind. Agatha regretted her outward charms, as she was only interested in living a life of prayer and contemplation, not gratifying the desires of men who were blind to the inner beauty of the soul.

Some of Agatha's suitors sought her hand in marriage, but a good number were only after sex. She put off one suitor after another, until one came along who would not be dissuaded. He was a successful politician—then, as now, apparently, an oversexed breed—named Quintianus, the governor of Sicily under the anti-Christian Roman emperor Decius. Quintianus did not believe in the subtle approach, nor was he what anyone would call a romantic. Having heard of Agatha's great beauty, not to mention her wealth, he issued a legal summons calling on her to report to him at Catania. She had no choice but to start out on the long journey from Palermo where she lived. When she left, a sense of dread came over her and she prayed for divine protection.

When Quintianus proposed marriage she turned him down flatly, drawing courage from her faith. He tried cajoling, then turned to bribery, then finally resorted to threats. When none of his gambits worked, in a fit of rage he had her dispatched to a whorehouse, run by a woman he knew, where Agatha would be forced to lose her virginity. This banishment was also intended as a punishment for Agatha's stubbornness in remaining a Christian. Before she went to the dreaded house of ill repute, Agatha prayed to God, asking Him to preserve her chastity. Despite the repeated sexual assaults she experienced in the brothel, her prayer to remain undefiled was answered.

The doctor then revealed himself to be none other than St. Peter, and the apparition healed her mangled flesh in an instant.

Eventually, Quintianus went over the deep edge and commanded the madam to cut off Agatha's breasts. The wicked brothel keeper executed the deed without hesitation. When a doctor willing to reattach her breasts visited the wretched and agonized Agatha, she refused. Agatha declared that she didn't want any medical attention, and that God would take care of her. The doctor then revealed himself to be none other than St. Peter, and the apparition healed her mangled flesh in an instant.

Nevertheless, the beleaguered Agatha didn't live much longer. Quintianus had her shuttled back and forth between the brothel and jail, and after repeated tortures Agatha's will to live left her. While being rolled on the ground naked over broken crockery, she prayed to God to end her sufferings and take her. She promptly died, pure to the end, in the year 251. Her canonization date has been lost to time, but it is believed to have been in the early part of the fifth century.

In 253, Agatha came to Catania's rescue when the massive volcano Mt. Etna erupted, threatening to bury the town under tons of red-hot lava.

Despite her death, Agatha's activities were far from over. In 253, Agatha came to Catania's rescue when the massive volcano Mt. Etna erupted, threatening to bury the town under tons of red-hot lava. The people took hold of a veil that had belonged to the saint and paraded it around the town, chanting prayers all the while. Miraculously, the lava flow split in two, each river of liquid fire going down a valley on either side of Catania, leaving the city untouched. As for the veil, it mysteriously changed color. The next time it was needed, in 1444, the veil halted Etna's flow again, but unfortunately it didn't work so well in 1669, and an eruption of Etna that year nearly obliterated Catania. In 1743, Agatha's veil was successfully deployed against the black plague, which had savaged the population of the neighboring city of Messina. Thankful for her posthumous aid over the centuries, the people of Catania hold a celebration every February 2 to 4, during which they push huge wooden candelabra through the streets, amid blasts of fireworks, and carry a gilded silver bust of St. Agatha about on a bier.

St. Agatha is frequently depicted carrying her severed breasts on a platter. In modern times, she is considered to be the patron saint of breast cancer patients. Perhaps oddly, she is also the patron of foundry workers, on the logic that foundry workers make bells, and bells are shaped more or less like breasts. (So, for instance, the Catholic association of bellringers is called the Guild of St. Agatha.) Due to her power to defeat the destructive power of volcanoes, she is prayed to for protection from fire and lightning, and likewise the fact that she provided safety from the dangers emanating from a mountain causes her to be beloved by alpinists, who look to her for help.

MIRACLES
OF
ST. AGATHA

Staying chaste
while in a whorehouse

Having her severed
breasts reattached

Stopping the eruption
of Mt. Etna

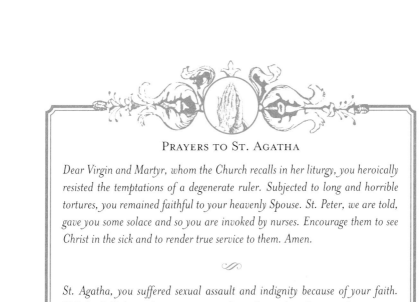

PRAYERS TO ST. AGATHA

Dear Virgin and Martyr, whom the Church recalls in her liturgy, you heroically resisted the temptations of a degenerate ruler. Subjected to long and horrible tortures, you remained faithful to your heavenly Spouse. St. Peter, we are told, gave you some solace and so you are invoked by nurses. Encourage them to see Christ in the sick and to render true service to them. Amen.

St. Agatha, you suffered sexual assault and indignity because of your faith. Help heal all those who are survivors of sexual assault and protect those women who are in danger. Amen.

St. Anthony of Padua

PATRON SAINT *of*
✳ FINDING LOST OBJECTS ✳

T. ANTHONY OF PADUA was not actually from Padua; he was Portuguese, born and raised in Lisbon. He was a compassionate and humble man, a true heir of his teacher, St. Francis of Assisi. Today, probably no saint is as beloved as he is or receives as many prayers as he does. That's partly because St. Anthony is the patron saint of finding lost objects—and who hasn't experienced the dislocating sensation of losing something, from a set of keys or a wallet to something truly irreplaceable—and partly because he was one of the greatest miracle workers (or "thaumaturgists") the Church has ever known. He was also gentle and devout, like his mentor, St. Francis of Assisi.

Originally named Fernando, Anthony was born in 1195 to parents of noble family. It has been said that his father was descended from no less a personage than Godfrey of Bouillon, the leader of the First Crusade. Whether or not this is true, by the time he was fifteen young Fernando decided to devote his life to the Church in a less secular fashion than his alleged forebear had. He left home to join the convent of St. Vincent, near Lisbon, as a member of an order called the Canons Regular of St. Augustine. Soon, in search of even deeper solitude, he moved on to another convent, in Coimbra, where he could concentrate on studying theology and living a life of contemplation and devotion.

In 1220 while still at the convent, Fernando witnessed something that would change his life: the bodies of some Franciscan friars who had been murdered—martyred—while preaching Christianity to the Moroccans, known in those days as Moors. He was so impressed by the slain friars' devotion that he left the Canons Regular and joined the Franciscans, taking the name of Anthony. He went straight to Morocco hoping to convert the Moors, or at least to die trying. That was not his destiny, however, and he accomplished neither goal. After only a short time among the Arabs he fell ill and had to sail back to Europe.

As soon as he was well, Anthony went to Assisi for a general meeting of the Franciscans. While he was there he kept a low profile. So low, in fact, that no one had any idea of his potential. He was assigned to be the priest at the hermitage of Monte Paolo, near Forli in Italy. Then, one day his moment came and he no longer hid his light under a bushel. A group of Franciscan and Dominican friars came to Monte Paolo for ordination, and Anthony was called on to preach to them. He started out awkwardly, but within minutes he showed himself to be a spellbinding orator, an eloquent and persuasive advocate of Christian doctrine. The fact that he was handsome and had a commanding voice only added to his charisma.

Anthony had found his calling, and spent the rest of his short life—he died when he was only thirty-six years old—as a teacher and preacher. He could be hard-hitting and even harsh in his attacks on false beliefs, to the point where he was nicknamed "the hammer of the heretics." He attracted a lot of attention for another reason as well: miracles of all kinds seemed to happen whenever Anthony was around.

Once in Rimini, a horse refused his oats, fasted for three days, and finally knelt down to adore the Blessed Sacrament that Anthony was holding. When some heretics, who had probably been smashed once too often by the "hammer," decided to get revenge by poisoning him, the young Franciscan just made the sign of the Cross and consumed the noxious platter without ill effect. On several occasions, while Anthony was preaching outdoors, the people listening to him were miraculously kept dry even though it was pouring rain. They would have called him "the umbrella of the faithful" if umbrellas had been invented. Once when he was preaching, he predicted that the Devil would destroy the pulpit he was preaching from. Perhaps the man simply had a good eye for architectural weakness, but when the structure collapsed mid-sermon, he was miraculously preserved from any injury. Thankfully, no one in the congregation was hurt either.

> "The foot of him who kicks his mother deserves to be cut off!"
>
> —St. Anthony

Other strange events happened during Anthony's life. One time, he and a companion were traveling and stopped at the house of a poor woman, who offered them food and wine. Perhaps flustered by the presence of such a great spiritual figure, the woman left the tap of the wine keg open, and all the wine ran out. To make matters worse, Anthony's fellow Franciscan clumsily knocked over his glass, breaking it. But the thaumaturgic powers were active that day—the keg was suddenly full again and the glass reassembled itself so the saint could refresh himself.

In Padua, where Anthony lived during the last year of his life, the famous miracle of the amputated foot took place. A young miscreant named Leonardo forgot himself so far as to kick his own mother during an argument. Afterwards, in a fit of guilt, he went to Anthony and confessed. The saint, never one to suffer sin lightly, said, "The foot of him who kicks his mother deserves to be cut off!" He didn't mean it literally but Leonardo ran home and amputated his own foot. When Anthony heard about that, he rushed over and used his powers to reattach the extremity.

Anthony died in Padua after a short illness. Immediately thereafter, he appeared in a vision to the abbot of the convent where he had been staying. His sanctity was so obvious to so many people that less than a year after his death, in 1232, he was canonized by Pope Gregory IX, making his path to sainthood the shortest on record.

MIRACLES
OF
ST. ANTHONY OF PADUA

Eating poison without ill effect

Making a horse kneel and adore the Sacrament

Shielding disciples from rain

Reassembling broken wine glass and refilling empty wine keg

Reattaching miscreant's severed foot

PRAYER TO ST. ANTHONY OF PADUA

St. Anthony, perfect imitator of Jesus, who received from God the special power of restoring lost things, grant that I may find [mention your petition] which has been lost. At least restore to me peace and tranquility of mind, the loss of which has afflicted me even more than my material loss. To this favor I ask another of you: that I may always remain in possession of the true good that is God. Let me rather lose all things than lose God, my supreme good. Let me never suffer the loss of my greatest treasure, eternal life with God. Amen.

St. Augustine

PATRON SAINT of

* BREWERS *

S T. AUGUSTINE was born in A.D. 354 in what is now Algeria, and he was one of the greatest Africans who ever lived. He began his life as a reprobate, but by the time of his death he had become the supreme Christian scholar and religious teacher of his era.

In the fourth century, North Africa was part of the Roman Empire, which was already Christian. Nonetheless, many inhabitants of the area still adhered to some form of paganism. It was not so dissimilar from our world today. Political life was unstable and frightening, with the Roman Empire disintegrating and barbarians threatening to take over. Across all strata of society, people were searching for meaning and spirituality, but most didn't know where to find it. They flitted from one sect or movement to another, or chose to distract themselves with hedonism.

Augustine was one of these restless searchers. He came from a mixed background; his father, Patricius, was a pagan, and his mother, Monica (known to us as St. Monica) was a devout Christian. At his mother's behest, Augustine was raised as a Christian, although at first it didn't take. He fell away from the faith and lived an undisciplined youth, wasting his time drinking and partying.

As a teenager, Augustine drifted into petty crime. One night he and some friends broke into a pear orchard and stole some fruit. Augustine (he was no saint then!) wasn't interested in the pears, though. He confides in his autobiography, *The Confessions*, that he stole them out of sheer perversity. It just felt good to do what was wrong, to disobey the laws of man and God, he wrote.

Despite indications to the contrary, Augustine wasn't a thug in the making. He was an intellectual young man who wanted a career as an academic. He admitted that the pear episode was mainly due to bad company, that he wouldn't have done it alone and that his actions caused him shame. He applied himself to his studies, and his family managed to send him to college at Madaura, a city near his home. Augustine earned top grades and excelled at Latin (the Roman statesman Cicero was his idol). For graduate school, Augustine went on to Carthage, the cultural capital of North Africa, where his reputation as an orator and philosopher increased, along with the size of his ego.

"Conquer yourself and the world lies at your feet."

—ST. AUGUSTINE

While in Carthage, he fell in love with a woman and had a child with her, named Adeodatus. The as-yet-unsaintly Augustine didn't marry the woman, though, and continued to practice his wild after-hours lifestyle. Monica was deeply pained by her son's way of life, but she kept hoping that somehow, someday, she could make a difference and lead him onto the right path.

Meanwhile, Augustine had gotten heavily involved not with the Christian faith but with a religion that came from Persia and spread throughout the Greek and Roman world—Manichaeism. The Manichees believed that there were two equally strong powers in the world, good and evil, and that these entities were constantly duking it out, with victory never decisive. The whole visible universe was the battleground, including human beings, in whose souls the two eternal enemies contended. This religion taught that humans were totally powerless, and therefore they couldn't be blamed for any of the wrong they did. Augustine sank ten years of his life into Manichaeism, satisfying his overpowering need for self-justification.

Soon, Augustine's career as a professor of philosophy and Latin took him to Milan. It was far from home, but his mother went with him, having never lost faith in her son's potential. In Milan, he met the man who would change his life—St. Ambrose, the city's bishop, who is famous for, among many other achievements, being the first person in European history to read silently without moving his lips.

"I will suggest a means whereby you can praise God all day long, if you wish. Whatever you do, do it well, and you have praised God."

—ST. AUGUSTINE

One day, Augustine was walking by a walled garden, and something drew him inside. Sitting there, he heard a melodious child's voice saying, "Take up and read, take up and read." The closest book at hand was a copy of *St. Paul's Letters* and Augustine picked it up, opened it, and for the first time in his life really absorbed the Christian message with his heart as well as his mind. The passage his eye fell upon instructed the reader to live in imitation of Jesus.

In 387, he was baptized by St. Ambrose and returned to Africa, accompanied by his new wife, a Christian woman from a good family in Milan whom Monica had introduced him to and encouraged him to marry.

Once back home, Augustine was virtually drafted into the priesthood by popular acclaim, and spent the rest of his long life preaching Christianity and defending it against all challenges. Augustine particularly eschewed any form of Christianity that rejected anyone or taught a philosophy of exclusion. On his office wall a sign read, "Here we do not speak evil of anyone."

Augustine was made bishop of Hippo, a town near Carthage, an office he held for decades. He was a beloved figure in North Africa, known for his generous, inclusive philosophy that welcomed everybody in the Christian church. In his filled-to-capacity Sunday sermons, Augustine preached that the spirit was more important than the letter, that true inner devotion was more important than following rules. He died at the age of seventy-six, leaving a legacy of love and knowledge that is still vibrant. St. Augustine's canonization date is unknown.

Believe it or not, Augustine is the patron saint of brewers, in homage to the prodigious quantities of alcoholic beverages he consumed in his pre-saintly days.

MIRACLES
OF
ST. AUGUSTINE

Swooping down from heaven to rescue a falling baby before it met an untimely demise, and subsequently returning the child to astonished onlookers

PRAYER TO ST. AUGUSTINE

You were a sensuous man who was often tormented by natural appetite and desire. You found your way to God through your stronger desire to live a spiritual life rich with meaning. Help me to see as you taught, that God is present everywhere for those who are willing to seek Him, and for those who are willing to love Him as He loves us. Help me to see through my desires to God, and help me to see God's love for me in my desires. I ask you, St. Augustine, to help me find God in all that I see. Flood my spirit with the desire to know and love God with all my heart. Amen.

St. Barbara

PATRON SAINT of
* GOOD MARRIAGE * ARTILLERYMEN *
* PROTECTION FROM LIGHTNING *

ST. BARBARA, virgin and martyr, was born a pagan in the third century A.D. No one seems to know exactly where she was born, but it was a heathen country, and her father, Dioscorus, was a rich, powerful, and arrogant man. Barbara was nothing like him—from the earliest age she was inclined to contemplation and learning, and was devoted in particular to the study of religion. Of course, in her search for truth she studied pagan religion, since that was all she knew. As soon as she started delving into those beliefs and mysteries, her sharp critical sense and nascent spiritual wisdom told her that pagan religion was not the true path.

At first, logic led to her belief in one God, but before she could go the rest of the way toward the Christian faith she needed a teacher to explain revelation to her. Somehow, she heard of the great Church father Origen, who was then teaching and writing at Alexandria in Egypt. She wrote to him asking for guidance, and he sent Barbara a disciple named Valentinian to give her lessons and baptize her. Almost immediately after Barbara became a Christian, Christ appeared to her in a vision and said that He had chosen her to be his wife.

Barbara's father had other marital plans for her. He wanted her to marry for money and social position—an old story, though it was 1,700 years younger in the third century than it is now. She put him off, rejecting each suitor one by one, claiming that she wanted to stay single so that she could take care of dear old dad in his declining years. Dioscorus wasn't happy, but he agreed to wait a while. He couldn't tolerate even for a minute, however, his daughter's involvement with this bizarre new cult, Christianity. Domestic conflict ensued, with quarrels and displays of defiance large and small. For example, Barbara's room had two windows and against Dioscorus' wishes she had a third installed to symbolize the Trinity. That window was a constant reproach to him.

Before he went off on a business trip, Dioscorus moved Barbara's bedroom to an isolated tower of their mansion and planted several idols there, in the hope that their presence would bring her back to her former more acceptable pagan ways. Imagine Dioscorus' shock when upon his return, he found the idols shattered to bits and strewn around the room. He exploded with fury, causing Barbara to flee the house in terror. She ran off to the woods and holed up in a cavern, where she lived and prayed in peace. The surrounding vegetation, as if guided by divine will, grew around the entrance to the cavern, hiding the future saint within from prying eyes.

Eventually, her father mobilized the neighborhood to look for her by offering a bounty to anyone who could bring the young girl back home. Some shepherds caught sight of Barbara one day when she ventured out of her rustic hideaway; they seized her and delivered her to her father. If they had known what he was about to do, they might not have been so eager.

Dioscorus brought his own flesh and blood before a civil court and denounced her for disobedience. Barbara was brutally tortured—twice—and when the secret bride of Christ refused to go back on her faith, she was sentenced to death. Dioscorus, believe it or not, volunteered to strike the deathblow himself. No sooner had he done so, sending his own daughter to heaven, than a bolt of lightning zigzagged out of the clear blue sky and incinerated both him and the judge. Both of their souls were dispatched directly to hell.

Barbara was brutally tortured—twice—and when the secret bride of Christ refused to go back on her faith, she was sentenced to death.

St. Barbara is prayed to for a good, happy marriage because of her spiritual marriage to Christ—the fact that she never married a human being on earth is beside the point. She is also invoked for protection from lightning, and by those who are in danger of dying without receiving the last sacraments.

A famous story has it that in the mid-16th century, St. Stanislaus Kostka, a young Pole with ambitions to become a priest, became critically ill on a journey and had to stop in the house of a Protestant, who didn't want the sacraments performed on his premises. St. Stanislaus prayed to St. Barbara, and she appeared to him as a beautiful young virgin accompanied by two angels. She gave him the sacrament herself and he recovered, going on to join the Jesuits. A similar incident occurred in 1448, when a man in Germany named Henry Kock was trapped in a burning house. He prayed to St. Barbara, and her appearance gave him the strength to escape the blaze and remain alive until he could receive the sacrament.

Interestingly, St. Barbara is also the patron saint of artillerymen, which came about this way: because her murder was instantly avenged by lightning, St. Barbara is invoked by the righteous against death by lightning and, by extension, fire and explosions. When gunpowder was introduced to Europe from China in the 15th century it often blew up unexpectedly, causing the primitive guns and cannon to kill their operators instead of the enemy. Naturally, the nervous soldiers called upon St. Barbara for protection. Today, in the United States, the Order of St. Barbara is an honorary military society that bestows its recognition on particularly distinguished members of the artillery corps of the Army and Marines. It is based in Fort Sill, Oklahoma.

St. Barbara is usually depicted in a three-windowed room, carrying a palm frond symbolizing martyrdom, and is believed to have been canonized in the early eighth century.

MIRACLES

OF

ST. BARBARA

✝

Plants moved by themselves to hide her from view

Lightning struck down those who killed her

Appearing in later centuries to those who are in danger of death without receiving sacraments

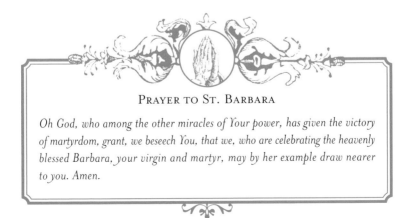

PRAYER TO ST. BARBARA

Oh God, who among the other miracles of Your power, has given the victory of martyrdom, grant, we beseech You, that we, who are celebrating the heavenly blessed Barbara, your virgin and martyr, may by her example draw nearer to you. Amen.

St. Clare of Assisi

PATRON SAINT of
✳ TELEVISION ✳ TELEVISION WRITERS ✳

ST. CLARE OF ASSISI came from a noble Italian family. She was born in 1194 in Assisi, the daughter of Favorino Scifi, the count of Sasso-Rosso, and the countess Ortolana. Like many other saints before and after her, Clare's spiritual life began with rebellion against her parents, even though they, too, were devout Christians.

When Clare was eighteen, she saw a priest (soon to be known as St. Francis) preaching in the streets of Assisi, and decided to emulate him in rejecting worldly things and living an unencumbered life of joyful poverty. She introduced herself and they became close friends. Francis saw right away that Clare was a kindred spirit and decided to help her reach her goal of ascetic piety. On Palm Sunday, 1212, the decisive moment arrived. When all the other worshippers in the Cathedral of Assisi went up to the altar rail to receive their palm fronds, Clare stayed behind. In her state of ecstasy, she was totally unaware of what was going on around her and remained seated. The priest, sensing Clare's religious awakening, rewarded her by personally delivering the palm frond to her during the service.

That night, Clare sneaked out of her family's house and went to the Portiuncula, the tiny, ramshackle chapel where Francis and his friars gathered. Realizing that before him was the woman who would found the female equivalent of the Franciscan order, Francis gave her a rough, brown habit just like his, tied it on with a cord of rope, and chopped off her hair. Then and there, Clare took a vow of lifelong poverty in the service of Christ.

The first place she went in her new life of religious devotion was the Benedictine abbey of San Paolo, where her father, Count Favorino, came to visit her. He was appalled to see his daughter living a life of poverty and celibacy instead of marrying someone of her family's choosing and taking her place in society. He was a forceful man—though not a cruel one, as so many fathers of saints seem to have been—but even his best efforts couldn't shake Clare's resolve. Like plenty of teenage girls, she was intense and headstrong, but unlike most, she had staying power.

Soon Francis found her a place in the small chapel of San Damiano, outside Assisi, which had been the scene of his own conversion experience. He had used a good deal of his family money to rebuild it, and now the humble structure found its destiny. It was to be the headquarters of a new order of sisters, the Poor Clares, otherwise known as the Order of Poor Ladies. Soon, Clare's sister Agnes (later St. Agnes) ran away from home, too, and joined the order. Eventually, her younger sister Beatrix, her Aunt Bianca and her mother Ortolana joined the Poor Clares as well. Sainthood may run in the Sasso-Rosso family, as Ortolana is close to sainthood herself. She has been honored by the Church with the title of Blessed, which is one step away from canonization.

Clare received a special dispensation from the Pope giving the sisters of her order permission to subsist entirely on begging, so that they could adhere fully to the principle of spiritual poverty. Up until then, it had been thought improper for religious women to wander about freely, exposing themselves to the prying eyes and attentions of the public. Clare was above such concerns, and wanted her sisters to be just like Francis' friars, come what may.

"Go forth in peace, for you have followed the good road. Go forth without fear, for he who created you has made you holy, has always protected you, and loves you as a mother. Blessed be you, my God, for having created me."

—St. Clare of Assisi

Clare spent the rest of her long life (long for the Middle Ages, that is, at fifty-nine years) presiding over San Damiano as abbess. When Francis was ill and blind, she gave him shelter by building a little hut for him on the abbey's grounds. She was very solicitous of the sisters; documents tell how she used to go into their rooms at night and tuck in the ones who had kicked off the covers in their sleep. The sisters called her the "Seraphic Mother."

Clare, though humble and unassuming, performed many miracles. Once, this most pacific of women even repelled a military invasion using her God-given powers. In 1234 the Sicilian emperor Frederick II, laying waste to the valley around San Damiano, sent soldiers to scale the walls of the abbey and take it by storm. They had no idea what they were up against. As troops climbed in through her open window using a ladder, Clare grabbed a ciborium, a ritual container in which the host wafer is carried, and held it up to them. A blinding light emanated from it, and the dazzled invaders fell backward and plummeted to the ground. A little while later, the emperor sent another invasion force to the area, and this time Clare gathered all the sisters around her and asked them to kneel with her in prayer. As they did so, a wild windstorm whipped up and the soldiers fled, thoroughly demoralized.

A life of austerity and sacrifice takes a toll on anyone, even the pious, and Clare's last years were spent in a state of ill health. When she was too weak to go to Mass anymore, a live-action image of the service was miraculously projected onto the wall of her cell. For that reason, she is the patron saint of television—and also of television writers, though they are not known as a particularly devout breed. St. Clare is also invoked for help with vision problems and eye diseases. St. Clare died in 1253, and was canonized soon after in 1255.

MIRACLES
OF
St. Claire of Assisi

Repelling invaders with wind and blinding light

Seeing Mass taking place elsewhere while confined to her cell

PRAYERS TO ST. CLARE OF ASSISI

Oh blessed St. Clare, your life shines like a beacon and casts its light down the ages of the Church to guide the way to Christ. Look with compassion on the poor and humble who call on you for help. As you bow before your Eucharistic Lord in Heaven, speak to Him of my afflicted body and my broken spirit. Ask Him to heal me and to wash away my sins in his precious blood. Amen.

Holy and beloved saint, teach me to believe, as you did, that in the Blessed Eucharist I will find Jesus, who has only to say the word that I may be healed. Amen.

St. Dymphna

PATRON SAINT of
* PROTECTION FROM ANXIETY * MENTAL ILLNESS *

S̶T. DYMPHNA was born sometime before the fifth century A.D. in Ireland, which at the time was still partly pagan. Her father was the king of Oriel (for a small island, Ireland had a great many kings) and his wife was an exquisitely beautiful woman. Dymphna turned out to be as beautiful as her mother, so much so that after the queen died at an early age, the grief-stricken king (whose name may or may not have been Damon) decided that he would marry his own daughter. Naturally, she was disgusted by his unnatural advances, and decided to flee the rustic court.

After the queen died at an early age, the grief-stricken king decided that he would marry his own daughter.

Dymphna, unbeknownst to her father, had become a Christian, and she turned to a priest named Gerebernus or Gerebran (the good man's name is still debated to this day) for help, who advised her to sail with him across the English Channel to Belgium. They did this accompanied by the court jester and his wife, with the incestuous king in hot pursuit. Dymphna and Gerebernus took up residence in the chapel of St. Martin in the town of Gheel, near Antwerp. There they lived a Christian life and ministered to the needs of the poor and seekers of truth. Dymphna and Gerebernus became known and admired as holy people.

Their refuge was to be short-lived. The king's spies and messengers sniffed them out, reportedly by surveillance techniques that tracked their use of foreign coins, and reported back to the deranged ruler. When the king arrived in Gheel he confronted the Christian pair, and gave Dymphna one last chance to agree to the incestuous marriage. When Gerebernus protested, the king's henchmen killed him on the spot. Dymphna, undeterred, stood fast and refused to violate the laws of God and man. Writing the last chapter of this disturbing drama, the king cut off his daughter's head with his own hands. She was only fifteen years old. The date was May 15, sometime between 620 and 640.

Dymphna and her priestly protector were buried in a cave at Gheel, as was customary at the time. They remained buried for hundreds of years, and their story faded from memory. Then, in the 13th century, their bodies were exhumed, and the diggers were amazed to find them interred in sumptuously carved white marble sarcophagi that were so ethereal in their beauty, they looked as if they could only have been made by angels. That must have been the case, because the poor people of Gheel could never have afforded such luxury. The workmen also found a red brick carved with the Latin letters DYMPNA. That archaeological discovery gave rise to the veneration of St. Dymphna, who became the patron saint of the insane, most likely because her martyrdom came about at the hand of a presumably insane person.

From the time that the veneration of St. Dymphna began, sufferers of any mental disorder were said to be miraculously cured after praying at her grave. St. Dymphna is appealed to for delivery from the threat of mental illness in any of its forms, from psychosis to mild nervous conditions. In today's world, a prayer can be directed to St. Dymphna for relief from anxiety.

In today's world, a prayer can be directed to St. Dymphna for relief from anxiety.

The helpful, mentally soothing presence of St. Dymphna still hovers over Gheel today. Since the 13th century, which is also believed to be the time of her canonization, people afflicted with mental and nervous disorders have flocked to the town, drawn by the tales of miraculous cures effected by the saint. For many years there has been an insane asylum in the town, and long before the advances of modern psychiatry and psychology, patients there were treated with unusual kindness and subtlety. At this hospital, patients are placed under observation in an institutional setting, as in any conventional asylum. Subsequently, the patients are integrated into the community, placed in homes where they live and work peacefully alongside the locals, most of whom are farmers. The doctors monitor their progress secretly as the patients go about their daily tasks. If any of them should suffer a relapse, he or she is returned to the hospital until well enough to rejoin the community again. This colony for the mentally ill is unique in the world, and only with the total cooperation of all the town's residents could it work as it does.

In the United States today, there is a National Shrine of St. Dymphna in Massillon, Ohio, located on the grounds of a psychiatric hospital. The Shrine's literature states, "Although many have never heard of St. Dymphna, she is becoming increasingly popular in these days of worry, fear, and tension."

MIRACLES
OF
ST. DYMPHNA

Mental illness cured by praying at her grave

PRAYERS TO ST. DYMPHNA

We beg you, Lord, to hear the prayers of St. Dymphna on our behalf. Grant all those for whom we pray patience in their sufferings and resignation to your divine will. Please fill them with hope, and grant them the relief and cure they so much desire. Amen.

I turn to you, dear virgin and martyr, confident of your power with God and of your willingness to take my cause into your hands. I praise and bless the Lord for giving you to us as patron of the nervous and emotionally disturbed. I firmly hope that through your kind intercession He will restore my lost serenity and peace of mind. May He speak to my heart and reassure me: "My peace I give you. Let not your heart be troubled nor let it be afraid." Pray for me, dear St. Dymphna, that my nervous and emotional turmoil may cease, and that I may again know serenity and personal peace. Amen.

St. Francis of Assisi

PATRON SAINT of
* ANIMALS * ECOLOGY * MERCHANTS *

T. FRANCIS is probably the most universally acknowledged and best-loved saint in the history of Christianity, and the one about whose life the most is known, as his contemporaries wrote so much about him. Unlike some of his fellow saints, however, he wasn't born saintly. In fact, he started out life on the wrong path.

As he was growing, it became clear that Francis had a worldly side. He was attracted to the new love poetry of the French and Provençal troubadours, and in general to the art of gracious living. He had a warm, easygoing, magnetic personality that made everybody love him, indulge him, and forgive the faults that came from the flip side of his personality: laziness and a big ego. Francis was what today would be called a party animal, and hung out with a group of youths who took part in what was called in medieval times "riotous living." When he wasn't carousing, he managed to find time to work in his father's business, and did well at it.

Francis wasn't satisfied with painting the town red and making money; he also harbored dreams of military glory. When his home town of Assisi went to war with the neighboring city of Perugia, Francis signed on. The fight went badly for the Assisians; most were killed, and the Perugians only bothered to take prisoners from those families rich enough to pay ransom for their sons and fathers. Francis' ransom was paid, and he eventually made it back home a somewhat chastened man.

His next gambit for glory was to join the Fourth Crusade, one of the periodic European attempts to capture the Holy Land from the Muslims. Francis used his family's money to buy himself a horse, an impressive suit of armor and a richly decorated cloak. He rode off toward Jerusalem, but after only one day's journey something strange happened: he had a dream in which God told him he was dead wrong, 180 degrees off the right path, and should return home.

Francis obeyed the dream and went back to Assisi, where his former popularity finally failed him. He was universally mocked, and his father went crazy when he found out how much money Francis had wasted on outfitting himself for a war he had no intention of fighting. Even with this reception, something was starting to change in the young man. He didn't really care that no one supported him. He went off into the countryside to pray in solitude. One day Francis was riding along and saw a leper coming his way. He was naturally repulsed, but something made him get down off his horse. He kissed the leper on the hand, and the diseased man returned the kiss of peace. As Francis rode away overjoyed, he looked back and saw that the leper had disappeared.

Soon afterward he was praying for enlightenment in the old church at San Damiano when a crucifix spoke to him. It said: "Francis, restore my church." He thought this meant that he should pay for the rebuilding of the crumbling structure, so he took a great deal of money out of the family business and spent it on the project. When he found out, Francis' father finally snapped, and publicly disowned him. The local bishop mediated the conflict and told Francis to give the money back, that God would provide. Not only did Francis give the money back, but he also took his clothes off, leaving himself only a ragged undershirt, and fled to the forest singing. Thieves beat him, but he didn't care. Finally, he was free.

"Jesus is happy to come with us, as truth is happy to be spoken, as life to be lived, as light to be lit, as love is to be loved, as joy to be given, as peace to be spread."

—St. Francis of Assisi

Francis soon realized that what the voice he had heard at San Damiano meant was that he should restore the spirit of the whole Catholic Church, not just fix up one particular building. He became a preacher and just like before, people were drawn to him, only now it was for a different reason: they sensed his newfound holiness. Francis continued to love nature and poetry, as he had before his conversion, but now they were ways for him to get closer to God. He became known for his attunement to animals and his power over them. He preached to birds, who stopped singing and listened in silence, only flying away when he was finished speaking. When a wolf marauded around Assisi, killing people and livestock, Francis tamed the beast with a few words and glances. It never threatened anyone again and became a local mascot.

In time, the band of ragged preachers Francis had gathered around him numbered five thousand, and the group was formally accepted as an order by the Pope. They became the Friars Minor, now known as the Franciscan Friars. The friars continued to spread the message of radical poverty, but institutional woes caught up with them. Bureaucracy and dissent were taking their toll, to the point where Francis resigned his position as head of the order. He had never wanted to be in charge of anything; it just wasn't his style. The only two things this man of love hated were money and conflict.

In time, Francis was afflicted by illnesses both human and divine. He went blind, and the only way to save some of his sight was to have an operation that used hot irons on his face. He bore it quietly, saying that "brother fire" would spare him any discomfort. He then received the stigmata (the five wounds of Christ on the cross) which bled and caused great pain, not to mention great amazement to those who witnessed them. In 1226, St. Francis died at the age of forty-five, leaving behind an example of peace, love, and spontaneity that is still an inspiration and a challenge to us all. He was canonized a mere two years later in 1228, making his a swift journey to sainthood.

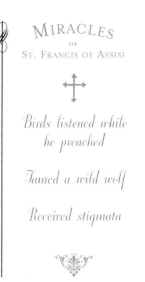

MIRACLES
OF
ST. FRANCIS OF ASSISI

Birds listened while he preached

Tamed a wild wolf

Received stigmata

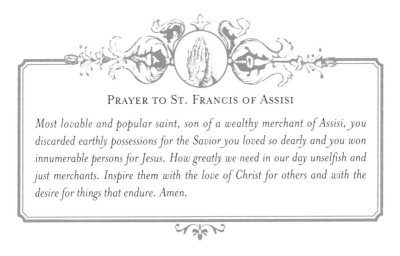

PRAYER TO ST. FRANCIS OF ASSISI

Most lovable and popular saint, son of a wealthy merchant of Assisi, you discarded earthly possessions for the Savior you loved so dearly and you won innumerable persons for Jesus. How greatly we need in our day unselfish and just merchants. Inspire them with the love of Christ for others and with the desire for things that endure. Amen.

St. Francis de Sales

PATRON SAINT of
★ JOURNALISTS ★ WRITERS ★

ST. FRANCIS DE SALES was born in France in 1567, during the religious wars sparked by the Protestant Reformation. He was destined to bring thousands of people back to the Catholic faith through his preaching and to inspire millions more through his writing. At first, he didn't appear to be cut out for such a historic role.

François de Sales de Boisy, known in English as Francis de Sales, was a quiet, diffident boy, inwardly sure of himself but unwilling to openly rebel. His family were aristocrats from Savoy, a part of France adjacent to Switzerland. Naturally, Francis' father wanted him to achieve worldly success and the cultivation befitting a gentleman. The young Francis was sent off to Paris to study the military arts, the first step to a career in government. Even though he felt he had a calling to the priesthood, Francis said nothing about it to his father, afraid of disappointing him. His next stop was Padua in Italy, where he earned a law degree. He continued to remain silent about his desire to join the priesthood. Even so, in the privacy of his own heart Francis was constantly praying, constantly seeking God's guidance.

Francis was preoccupied with the doctrine of predestination taught by some Protestants, to the point where hell and the afterlife were all he could think about. One day he had a crisis of faith, and prayed, "Oh Lord, if I am fated to spend eternity in hell, and in hell no one praises You, then grant me that I should at least praise You every moment that I am alive on this earth." Suddenly, Francis' fear lifted, and he was at ease for the first time in months. After this crisis of faith, he knew that the spiritual path was for him, and took a secret vow of celibacy. Soon afterward, Francis received a miraculous sign: While out riding, he fell off his horse three times, and each time it happened, his sword and scabbard clattered to the ground in such a way that they formed the sign of the Cross.

When his parents chose a bride for him, a girl from a rich and influential family, Francis realized that the time had come to tell everyone the truth. It was impossible for him to marry as he was destined for the Church. He also rejected his seat on the French Senate, for which he had been groomed by his father's political cronies. As a priest, he could have no hand in politics or other worldly matters. Instead, he asked another family friend, the bishop of Geneva, to ordain him and give him a job. The bishop did so, and Francis, newly appointed Provost of the Chapter of Geneva, got ready to walk into the lion's den. The year was 1593. Geneva at that time was the stronghold of Calvinism, a particularly harsh form of Protestantism, and Catholics were not welcome in the theocratic fortress city. Francis was undeterred. Having assigned himself the task of converting sixty thousand Genevans back to the Church of Rome, he took off for Switzerland with only his cousin Louis as his companion.

It was a bleak expedition. In the Calvinist territories, physical attacks on Catholics were common, and Francis was threatened with violence on many occasions. Even the animals around Geneva seemed to have it in for Catholics. A ravening wolf drove Francis up a tree, where he had to spend a particularly cold night tied to a branch to keep from falling off. In the morning, he was frozen to the tree and almost died. Some kind Genevans took him in, and before the future saint left their house they, too, had become Catholics.

Since the Protestants often didn't want to listen to his preaching, Francis came up with a revolutionary idea: He wrote short, inspiring, and elucidating essays on sheets of paper and slipped them under doorways or left them where people might find them and then read in private. Francis had invented the religious tract. Eventually, his tracts were collected in a book called *Introduction to the Devout Life*, which became hugely popular throughout Europe. One of the ideas Francis emphasized in his book was the importance of humor as a way of keeping things in perspective and deflating arrogance. He was humorous in real life, too. One day a threatening person challenged him, saying, "If I were to strike you on the cheek, what would you do?" He replied, "I know what I *should* do, but I cannot be sure of what I *would* do." The tolerant saint-to-be even approved of dancing!

Francis eventually brought many Protestants back to the Catholic Church, although not nearly as many as he would have

> *"Those who love God can never stop thinking about Him, longing for Him, aspiring to Him, and speaking about Him. If they could, they would engrave the name of Jesus on the hearts of all humankind."*
>
> —St. Francis de Sales

liked. He publicly debated the chief Protestant theologian of Geneva, Theodore Beza, but Beza didn't convert. Nonetheless, Francis' reputation spread, and having survived his mission to Switzerland he became a sort of international preaching star. His learned but accessible sermons were popular with kings, popes, and ordinary people alike. He kept writing, too, and thanks to his voluminous output of persuasive, popular writings, he is the patron saint of journalists and writers.

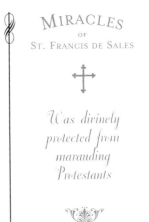

MIRACLES
OF
ST. FRANCIS DE SALES

Was divinely protected from marauding Protestants

It was while on the lecture circuit that he met the woman who was to be his partner in the creation of a new religious order. Jeanne de Chantal, a widow who was somewhat infirm, approached Francis and told him of her ambition to found an order for women who wanted to serve God but were too weak or ill to tolerate convent life. He helped her start the order of Visitation Nuns. Jeanne, an ecstatic mystic, inspired Francis to become more mystical in his own spiritual life. Eventually, Jeanne was also canonized and is known as St. Jeanne de Chantal.

Francis' exhausting work took its toll on his health. In 1622, he suffered a stroke and died a few days later. The last word he spoke was, "humility." St. Francis was canonized by Pope Alexander VII thirty-four years later, in 1665.

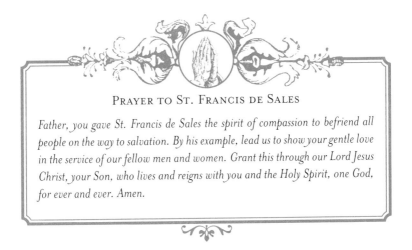

PRAYER TO ST. FRANCIS DE SALES

Father, you gave St. Francis de Sales the spirit of compassion to befriend all people on the way to salvation. By his example, lead us to show your gentle love in the service of our fellow men and women. Grant this through our Lord Jesus Christ, your Son, who lives and reigns with you and the Holy Spirit, one God, for ever and ever. Amen.

St. Gerard Majella

PATRON SAINT of
* EXPECTANT MOTHERS *

ST. GERARD MAJELLA is the wonder-working thaumaturge of the 18th century. Even among the select group of saints who have made the spiritual grade, the thaumaturge is a rare breed. Defined as "a saint who works miracles not just occasionally, but as a matter of course," thaumaturges come along, it is said, only once a century.

Born in 1726 to a humble family in the south of Italy, near Naples, Gerard seemed destined for a working-class existence. His father, Dominic Majella, was a tailor. Dominic died when his son was twelve, leaving the family in dire poverty. Gerard's mother was forced to apprentice him to a tailor in order to support the family. The master tailor was not a bad man, but the shop foreman treated Gerard cruelly. Tailoring seemed to be a dead end for Gerard.

Gerard was already very pious and had hopes of joining the priesthood. Due to his delicate health, which may have been the result of the extreme physical penances he imposed on himself even as a boy, he was rejected as unfit by all the religious orders he applied to. The closest he could get to the priestly life was to become the household servant of a priest. He did just that.

The priest he worked for proved no more pleasant to be around than the tailor's foreman, and once again, as is the lot of so many saints, Gerard was underappreciated and abused. He hung on in spite of his poor treatment, humbly doing his duty for several years until the priest died. Gerard then returned to his erstwhile trade, darning doublets and hemming hose as he had done before, only this time in his own shop.

Gerard still harbored hope that he might join an order, renounce worldly pursuits, and devote his life to helping people and propagating the faith. He asked the Franciscans to let him be a novice and was refused. Other orders did likewise. Finally, the Redemptorists accepted him as a lay brother in 1749, when he was twenty-three years old. He had only six years left to live.

Among the Redemptorist brethren, Gerard soon acquired a well-deserved reputation for sanctity and obedience. His tasks at the convent were mainly menial—he was a gardener, sacristan, and porter, and also used his tailoring skills to mend the brethren's garments. He was always volunteering to do the work of others and anticipated the wishes of superiors rather than having to be told what to do. His obedience began to reach miraculous proportions. On one occasion, a visiting brother was given a demonstration by one of Gerard's superiors. He sent the young man on an errand and told the visitor that he would make Gerard return by just thinking it. Sure enough, Gerard heard the command in his heart and immediately turned back to the convent.

Gerard's wonder-working had actually begun much earlier in his life. When he was just five years old, he used to pray before a statue of the Virgin and Child in his town's church. The infant Jesus would come down from the statue and give the boy little buns to eat. His family didn't believe him when he told them where the buns came from, but one day his sister went to spy on him and saw him receive the supernatural snack. At the age of seven, the parish priest denied him Communion at the altar rail because he was too young, so that night St. Michael the Archangel himself appeared and brought Gerard the wafer.

The miracles happened so frequently and attracted so much attention that finally his superiors told Gerard that he had to stop working wonders, or at the very least to get clearance first.

As an adult, Gerard's miracles came fast and furious. He was constantly bilocating (appearing in more than one place at once) and reading people's hearts and minds. He also had a knack for getting pennies from heaven. One day, he led a group of students on a pilgrimage to a nearby mountain where the archangel Michael had once appeared. They ran out of money, so Gerard prayed for help. Soon, someone offered to put them up in his house for the night, and when the pilgrims set out the next morning, another person approached Gerard and handed him a big roll of bills.

The miracles happened so frequently and attracted so much attention that finally Gerard's superiors told him that he had to stop working wonders, or at the very least to get clearance first. One day, he happened to be walking by a scaffold on the side of a building when a workman fell off. Gerard used his thaumaturgic power to stop him in midair. With the man in suspended animation, the future saint ran off to the convent to get permission to save his life. It was granted immediately, and Gerard unfroze the workman and let him drift gently and safely down to earth.

Gerard's biggest trial came from a rather unexpected quarter. A young woman brazenly accused him of getting her pregnant, and because of the Redemptorist rules against brothers defending themselves in public, he had to let the accusation stand and say nothing at all. Always ready to assume the worst, even about a holy man, the townspeople gossiped and whispered about him. Even the superior of the order was convinced of Gerard's lustful guilt. Finally, the woman admitted she had been put up to it. This association with pregnancy, perhaps paradoxically, has caused Gerard to be the patron saint of expectant mothers.

In 1755, at the age of twenty-nine, Gerard Majella died of tuberculosis. He had predicted the exact day and hour of his death. St. Gerard's canonization took place nearly two centuries later. His is one of the few canonization dates for which we know the exact day he achieved sainthood, December 11th, 1904.

MIRACLES
OF
ST. GERARD MAJELLA

✝

Bilocation

Mind reading

*Procuring money
and food from
supernatural sources*

*Suspending a man
in midair*

*Predicting the day
and hour of his death*

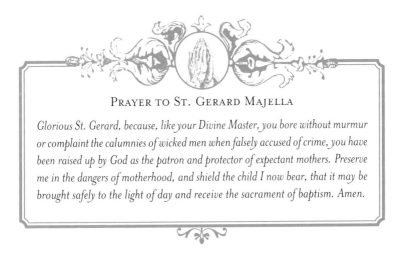

PRAYER TO ST. GERARD MAJELLA

Glorious St. Gerard, because, like your Divine Master, you bore without murmur or complaint the calumnies of wicked men when falsely accused of crime, you have been raised up by God as the patron and protector of expectant mothers. Preserve me in the dangers of motherhood, and shield the child I now bear, that it may be brought safely to the light of day and receive the sacrament of baptism. Amen.

St. Joseph

PATRON SAINT *of*

* HOUSE HUNTING *

* GETTING A GOOD PRICE FOR ONE'S HOUSE *

T. JOSEPH was the husband of Mary the mother of Christ. Although, of course, he wasn't Jesus' actual biological father, St. Joseph was a father to him in every other way. He raised Jesus, brought him up in the Jewish tradition as a good Jewish father should, and taught him the carpentry trade. Church tradition calls him the foster father of Our Lord.

Although he made his living as a carpenter, Joseph was actually of royal lineage, a descendant of King David. Like Jesus, he was born in Bethlehem, which was formerly the capital city of the Jewish kings. At some point he moved to Nazareth, where he met Mary and asked her to marry him. (Some legends have it that Joseph had been married before, and even that he was extremely old at the time he met Mary, but these stories are doubtful.) While they were engaged, he found out that Mary was pregnant. Needless to say, Joseph was shocked, embarrassed, and angry, but his natural refinement prevented him from making a public scandal, or even getting into a fracas with Mary over this outrageous problem. Instead, he planned to go ahead with the marriage and then quietly divorce her, as Jewish law allowed. Before Joseph could do the deed he had a vision, or rather a visitation. An angel appeared and told him that Mary had miraculously conceived while remaining a virgin. Reassured, though somewhat mystified, Joseph married her.

Although he made his living as a carpenter, Joseph was actually of royal lineage, a descendant of King David.

From the beginning, it was clear that the marriage was going to be an eventful one. Just before Jesus' birth, Joseph and Mary had to report to Bethlehem to be counted in a census imposed by the Roman emperor, Caesar Augustus. Joseph was under a great deal of stress because the nine-months-pregnant Mary was in no condition to travel, and due to the influx of people in town for the census, all the inns had their "No Vacancy" signs out. Thankfully, Joseph was nothing if not a steady, responsible, and capable husband. He used his ingenuity and persuasiveness and (with Divine help, of course) found shelter in a private house in Bethlehem (not a stable, as is commonly believed), where the Nativity took place.

It didn't take long for news to get out about this miraculous birth. Wise men from the East dressed in exotic garb and bearing gifts, were seen in the neighborhood. People whispered that the baby might be the next King of the Jews. When Joseph and Mary eventually took the infant Jesus to be presented to the priests in the Temple of Jerusalem (as was customary for the sons of members of the Jewish priestly caste, of which Joseph was one), the high priest declared that Jesus would be "a light to shine upon the nations." When the local Roman puppet king, a petty tyrant named Herod the Great, got wind of the rumors, he smelled a rival, and resolved to fix the problem. Because he had no idea which baby everyone was talking about, and of course no right-minded person would tell him, he decided to kill all the male babies under the age of two, just to make sure. Clearly, Herod had not yet mastered analytical thinking. Warned by an angel of the impending threat, Joseph had a new task: to save his family from the Massacre of the Innocents.

The Holy Family fled to Egypt under cover of night, where they found refuge for several years. When the persecution ended and Herod's brutal attentions turned to other things, Joseph and his family returned to Nazareth. There, Joseph resumed his carpentry business and the education of his foster son, and life was quiet for a while. Joseph was a devout Jew; in a prayer in the Passover service, Jews express the hope that they will celebrate the holiday "next year in Jerusalem." For the zealous Joseph, Passover was celebrated in Jerusalem every year. It was on one of those trips, when Jesus was twelve, when a notable event in the family's life together occurred. While Joseph and Mary were walking through the crowded streets, they suddenly realized that Jesus was missing. In a panic, Joseph and Mary searched everywhere for three days. Finally, they found Jesus, safe and sound, sitting before the learned elders in the Temple, lecturing them while they listened humbly.

Mary, most likely feeling both relieved and angry, said, "Your father and I have been looking for you everywhere! What were you doing?" Jesus replied, "Didn't you know I have to be about my father's business?" Joseph must have heard these words with very mixed emotions. On the one hand, he rejoiced in the fact that Jesus was beginning his mission on earth, fulfilling his destiny as Savior of mankind. On the other hand, Jesus' uncompromising words were meant to remind Joseph that he wasn't his real father. Joseph, being the saintly man he was, accepted it with equanimity.

Joseph's role was over, and fittingly, we read no more of him in the Bible after this stage of Jesus' life. Presumably, he died before Jesus' public mission began. Even though there is no record of his canonization, St. Joseph, the quiet man of the gospels, is venerated today as the patron of the Church, and his statue can be found in front of just about every Catholic church in the world.

Thanks to his trade as a carpenter and his skill at finding lodging for his family, St. Joseph is also the patron saint of house hunting.

MIRACLES
OF
ST. JOSEPH

✝

St. Joseph did not perform any miracles during his lifetime, but it is safe to say that his kindness and love for Mary and Jesus were miracles in their own right. Without St. Joseph's miraculous compassion, we could only speculate the dark fate that Mary and her unborn child would have faced.

PRAYERS TO ST. JOSEPH

Oh St. Joseph, whose protection is so great, so strong, so prompt before the throne of God, I place in you all my interests and desires. Amen.

Oh St. Joseph, assist me by your powerful intercession, and obtain for me from your divine Son all spiritual blessings through Jesus Christ, Our Lord; so that having engaged here below your heavenly power I may offer my thanksgiving and homage to the most loving of fathers. Amen.

St. Jude

PATRON SAINT *of*

* LOST OR DESPERATE CAUSES *

S̲T. JUDE, the patron saint of desperate causes, so well known from the classified sections of the newspapers, was actually Jesus' first cousin. He and his brothers, St. James the Less and St. Simon the Zealot, were the sons of Cleophas, the brother of St. Joseph. In first-century Palestine, families were close and relations were described a little more informally than today; hence Jude and his brothers are often referred to as the "brethren" of Jesus. In any case, Jude is said to have looked a lot like Jesus.

Jude was most likely a fisherman by trade, and was one of the original twelve apostles who preached the message of Jesus in Judea, Samaria, and elsewhere in the Holy Land. An invitation from a king led him to travel even farther. Abagaro, the ruler of Edessa, in Syria, suffered from leprosy and had heard of Jesus' miraculous powers, so he invited the Savior to come and heal him. Instead of going in person, Jesus dispatched Jude and gave him a cloth that he had pressed against his face, leaving a miraculous image. It could be said that this picture of Jesus was the first photograph ever made! The king was inspired by this likeness and became a Christian. Of course, the fact that his leprosy was cured didn't hurt, either. To this day, in commemoration of the power of that image, Jude is usually depicted bearing a portrait of Jesus in the form of a medallion worn around his neck.

Jude was most likely a fisherman by trade, and was one of the original twelve apostles who preached the message of Jesus in Judea, Samaria, and elsewhere in the Holy Land.

After the death of Jesus, Jude traveled widely throughout the Middle East in Syria, Armenia, Libya, and Persia. His brother Simon accompanied him on many of his missionary trips, and at first they were a big success. The two future saints impressed the king of Persia by subduing two crazed tigers who were terrorizing the locals. This feat impressed him so much, in fact, that he converted to Christianity. Following suit, sixty-thousand Persians joined the new faith along with him.

Unfortunately, as Jude and Simon penetrated farther into Asia, events took a turn for the worse. In Parthia (today's

Afghanistan, a trouble spot then, too, it seems) they ran into some pagans who were not sympathetic to the gospel, being under the sway of magicians who animated statues with evil spirits to make them appear to be gods. Jude exposed these idols for what they were by using his own miraculous powers to call the demons forth from the statues. They emerged, appearing in their true, hideous forms. The crowd remained hostile, though, as people often do when confronted by the evidence of their own mistakes. As Jude and Simon prayed for their salvation, the irate idolaters attacked them with clubs, knocking them unconscious. They then killed Jude and Simon by beheading them and shattering the severed orbs with an axe. Jude's body—whether with or without the head is unknown—was eventually brought to Rome, where it was placed in a crypt in St. Peter's Basilica. Some say it wasn't in Afghanistan that Jude was martyred but in Armenia. Some say he wasn't clubbed to death but shot with arrows, and some say that he died alone, not with Simon. Reports from two thousand years ago can sometimes be quite murky, but we do know that he was martyred for his true faith. Sadly, his canonization date is unknown.

St. Jude is also known for being the patron saint of lost causes. The most common explanation for this is that early believers confused his name with that of Judas—also called Iscariot—the traitorous apostle who gave Jesus up to the Romans.

Jude wrote one of the shorter books of the Bible, the Epistle of St. Jude. The Epistle is a letter he wrote to advise new Christians—especially Jewish converts—on how to resist the temptations of heresy—especially the Gnostics, the first-century equivalents of New-Agers. He uses pretty strong language against the heretics, calling them meteors that blaze brightly in the sky for a little while but then set forever in darkness.

St. Jude is also known for being the patron saint of lost causes. The most common explanation for this is that early believers confused his name with that of Judas—also called Iscariot—the traitorous apostle who gave Jesus up to the Romans. Whenever they wanted to pray to an apostle, they were advised to pick anyone other than Jude first. Poor St. Jude became a kind of lost cause himself! To make sure he isn't mistaken for the evil Judas—assigned by Dante to the lowest circle of hell—St. Jude is often called St. Jude Thaddeus. Another reason for his association with lost or desperate causes is the fact that he worked wonders, and was able to salvage seemingly impossible situations.

MIRACLES OF ST. JUDE

✝

Curing a king of leprosy with an image of Jesus

Subduing tigers

Revealing idols as demons

PRAYERS TO ST. JUDE

Most holy apostle, St. Jude, faithful servant and friend of Jesus, the Church honors and invokes you universally as the patron of hopeless cases, of things almost despaired of. Amen.

Pray for me, I am so helpless and alone. Make use, I implore you, of that particular privilege given to you, to bring visible and speedy help where help is almost despaired of. Amen.

Come to my assistance in this great need that I may receive the consolation and help of heaven in all my necessities, tribulations, and sufferings, particularly [here make your request] and that I may praise God with you and all the elect forever. Amen.

St. Lawrence

PATRON SAINT of
* COOKS * CHEFS * LIBRARIANS *
* PROTECTION AGAINST KITCHEN ACCIDENTS *

ST. LAWRENCE lived and died during the Dark Ages in Rome, and it is commonly believed that he was born in Toledo, Spain. For most people in Europe, the third century A.D. was a grim and chaotic time, and in Rome, the people were ruled by what would today be called a terrorist state. Rome was in a shambles, as barbarians (Goths and other fierce tribes) had literally battered down the gates and taken over. For Christians in particular it was a dark time, because the pagan barbarians were no more sympathetic to the Catholic faith than the old Romans had been. They would just as soon roast a Christian alive as look at him. On a dull day, the barbarian invaders might feed him or her to a lion or a wide array of other wild beasts.

With Christians reduced to living underground to escape the authorities and practice their religion undisturbed, no one was safe, not even the Pope. Back then, the Holy Father didn't go around in sumptuous white robes or get chauffeured in an armored car. Sixtus II, the pontiff at the time, was living in the catacombs like everyone else, and eventually, in the year 258, he was arrested and brought to stand trial. Lawrence was one of his seven deacons, and as Pope Sixtus went off to prison, Lawrence told him he would be bereft without his guidance. "Where are you hurrying off to, holy priest, without your deacon? Before, you never mounted the altar of sacrifice without me, your servant, and now you wish to do it without me." "Don't worry, Lawrence," the pope replied, "You'll be joining me within three days."

Since he knew he wouldn't be around for long, Lawrence decided to take all the money he had been saving up to feed the poor and distribute it immediately.

Since he knew he wouldn't be around for long, Lawrence decided to take all the money he had been saving up to feed the poor and distribute it immediately. When the Roman authorities got wind of this impending generosity, they confronted Lawrence and said, "We know there's more where that came from. Hand over all your treasure." Lawrence agreed, and within three days assembled all the poor, sick, and disabled people that the Christians sheltered and fed. The message was that they—not gold, silver, or gems—were the Church's real treasure. Needless to say, the barbarians were not amused. They arrested Lawrence on the spot and dragged him off to be tortured.

The prefect of Rome ordered the future saint to be roasted alive on a gridiron. Lawrence kept his equanimity throughout the fatal ordeal, perhaps aided by miraculous powers. He even had the presence of mind to joke about his predicament, telling the prefect, "I'm well-done on this side, you'd better turn me over!" Again, the Roman was reportedly not amused, but the Christians who witnessed this human barbecue were strengthened in their faith. Just before he died, Lawrence shouted out, "I'm cooked now!" His roasted head is preserved in a reliquary in the Vatican, and every year on his feast day, August 10th, the anniversary of his martyrdom, St. Lawrence's head is displayed to the faithful.

Just before he died, Lawrence shouted out, "I'm cooked now!" The Christians who witnessed this human barbecue were strengthened in their faith.

One treasure that Lawrence didn't hand over to the Romans was the Holy Chalice from which Jesus and the apostles had drunk their wine at the Last Supper. The saint managed to spirit the relic away to Spain, his native land, where it was kept safe in the town of Huesca. Over the centuries, the chalice passed from monastery to monastery, and eventually ended up in the Cathedral of Valencia, where pilgrims regularly seek it out. Made of carved, dark-red agate, the cup has a certificate of authenticity, written on parchment in the year 262 A.D. Some have confused it with the Holy Grail, the vessel that caught Jesus' blood as it dripped from his body on the Cross. In 1992, Pope John Paul II celebrated Mass with the Chalice in Valencia.

Immediately after his death, Lawrence's body was buried in the catacomb of St. Cyriaca on the Via Tiburtina in Rome. The Roman Emperor Constantine, whose conversion to Christianity brought the whole empire to the faith and made it repent of the anti-Christian mania that had killed Lawrence, built a little chapel to the martyr on that spot. Later on, the chapel was enlarged into a basilica, which is today known as San Lorenzo fuori le Mura (St. Lawrence outside the Walls). There are six other churches in Rome called San Lorenzo that are also dedicated to St. Lawrence. St. Lawrence had to wait a little longer to be canonized, which finally took place in 1881.

MIRACLES
OF
ST. LAWRENCE

Remaining unfazed while being roasted alive

Ever since San Lorenzo fuori le Mura was constructed, the faithful have gathered there to ask St. Lawrence to grant favors both large and small. Christians all over the world have appealed to St. Lawrence for help in a multitude of matters. His protection has particularly been sought against disasters and accidents in the kitchen, for obvious reasons. Similarly, St. Lawrence is the patron saint of cooks, not only professionals but also anyone who prepares meals in a kitchen. In that sense, he is a true household saint. St. Lawrence is also a patron saint for librarians, because in his capacity as a deacon he served as archivist for the underground Christian community in Rome. He is usually depicted carrying a gridiron, very much like the one on which he was martyred, with a palm leaf symbolizing martyrdom and a money purse for the alms he distributed to the poor.

PRAYER TO ST. LAWRENCE

Oh holy St. Lawrence, by God's ardent love, you exhibited faithful service to the Church and its treasures—the poor and the sick—and then attained a glorious martyrdom. Help us to love what you loved and to practice what you taught. Amen.

St. Martin de Porres

PATRON SAINT of
* BARBERS * HAIRSTYLISTS * THE LOVELORN *

T. MARTIN DE PORRES was born in Peru in 1579. His father was a Spanish nobleman and his mother was either an Inca or a freed African slave. Whatever the case may be, as a dark-skinned child of mixed ancestry, Martin was looked down upon by just about everybody. His father refused to acknowledge him as his son, and left the boy and his mother to fend for themselves.

Rather than making him angry and resentful, Martin's compromised status taught him humility. Right from the beginning, he learned not to value worldly distinctions and to see God in everyone. When his mother could no longer afford to support him, he was apprenticed to a surgeon, a lowly occupation in those times. (Sixteenth-century mothers tended not to use the words, "my son the doctor.") Many surgeons doubled as barbers, and Martin became an expert in that field, too. For this reason, he is the patron saint of barbers and hairstylists.

While practicing the tonsorial and medical arts, Martin was living a secret life of devotion. Every night, when the rest of the town was asleep, he would immerse himself in intense prayer and even flagellate himself three times to expiate his not-too-grievous sins. He also claimed to indulge in this self-mortification to hasten the conversion of pagans.

Before long, Martin had made up his mind to devote his entire life to God and to serving people in any way he could. He traveled to Lima and applied to the Dominican Convent of the Rosary. To his great joy he was accepted, and at the age of twenty-four was made a coadjutor brother. Martin's assignment was to the infirmary, where he dispensed medical care first to his fellow Dominicans and eventually to all. He became famous throughout the city for his gentleness and patience, and for the special way he had of healing and comforting. The gentle brother even ministered to ailing cats and dogs.

It soon became apparent to those who knew him that Martin de Porres was more than just a nice, humble barber, doctor, and veterinarian-about-town. Strange and wonderful things had a way of happening around him. If medicine wasn't available, he could make water work just as well. If he felt he was needed somewhere, walls were no barrier. When sixty novices who had taken a vow to remain locked away in a distant part of the convent complex became severely ill, Martin simply passed through the locked doors and cured them. He developed a talent for bilocation, or being in more than one place at a time. When a Lima businessman got sick on a trip to Mexico, he said to himself, "I wish Martin were here to help me." Almost immediately, the godly barber-surgeon walked through the door, although he had never left Lima.

In time, Martin's bilocation reached globetrotting proportions. He was spotted in Africa, in China, and even in Japan. Thanks to the power of miracles, he could heal worldwide without leaving home. A chained and shackled slave in Africa received a visit from Martin, who spoke to him and his fellow slaves about Christ and the Church. The slave was eventually purchased by a Spaniard and brought to Peru, and when he saw Martin there, asked him if he had had a good voyage. Martin hadn't had any voyage at all—at least not on a ship.

Martin had other unusual powers. He always seemed to have ready cash to give alms to the poor and made it a point to feed approximately one hundred indigent people each day. If the gentle Dominican was so poor, where was the money coming from? Martin wasn't robbing banks. The funds came to him via supernatural financing.

He sometimes flouted convention and incurred the displeasure of his superiors at the convent. Once, Martin came across a destitute man covered with weeping sores. The man, being homeless, had nowhere to stay so Martin brought him to the convent and let him sleep in his own bed. One of the other Dominican brothers said this wasn't appropriate, to which Martin replied, "Compassion, my dear brother, is preferable to cleanliness. Reflect that with a little soap I can easily clean my bed covers, but even with a torrent of tears I would never wash from my soul the stain that my harshness toward the unfortunate would create."

On another occasion, Martin took in a townsperson who had been stabbed in a street fight, and kept him at the convent until there

> *"Compassion, my dear brother, is preferable to cleanliness. Reflect that with a little soap I can easily clean my bed covers, but even with a torrent of tears I would never wash from my soul the stain that my harshness toward the unfortunate would create."*
>
> —St. Martin de Porres

was room for him in a hospice kept by the future saint's sister (charity, it seems, ran in the family). One brother was scandalized, but Martin set him straight by saying, "Forgive my error, and please instruct me, for I did not know that the precept of obedience took precedence over that of charity." The brother never made that mistake again!

In addition to his work with the poor and sick, Martin was known for solving problems for the lovelorn. When his niece's upcoming marriage was jeopardized because she didn't have a dowry, Martin came up with the money for her within three days; he helped his sister and her husband resolve their marriage problems, too. That's why today, his assistance is invoked where affairs of the heart are concerned, particularly in Latin American countries.

Martin de Porres died in 1639 at the age of sixty, and was canonized nearly three hundred years later, in 1962. Not only is he the patron saint of barbers, but he is also an inspiration to those who are trying to solve the world's ongoing problems of ill health and racial injustice.

MIRACLES
OF
ST. MARTIN DE PORRES

Bilocation

Healing with water instead of medicine

Procuring money of divine origin

PRAYER TO ST. MARTIN DE PORRES

To you, St. Martin de Porres, we prayerfully lift up our hearts filled with serene confidence and devotion. Mindful of your unbounded and helpful charity to all levels of society and also of your meekness and humility of heart, we offer our petitions to you. Pour out upon our families the precious gifts of your solicitous and generous intercession; show to the people of every race and every color the paths of unity and of justice; implore from our Father in heaven the coming of his kingdom, so that through mutual benevolence in God men may increase the fruits of grace and merit the rewards of eternal life. Amen.

St. Monica

Patron Saint of
MOTHERS *RELATIONSHIP ADVICE*
ALCOHOLICS *THOSE WHO ARE ABUSED*

S|T. MONICA is not only a saint but also the mother of a saint, St. Augustine. Not surprisingly, she is the patron saint of mothers. She is also appealed to for relationship advice since she successfully arranged a happy marriage for her son, an unwed father in love with an unsuitable woman.

Born in A.D. 333 in what is now Algeria, Monica was raised a Christian. Nevertheless, for financial reasons her parents married her off to a pagan government official, Patricius. He was much older than she, and his irreligious ways went hand in hand with a notoriously bad temper. As if that weren't trial enough, Patricius' mother lived with them and proved to be an extremely difficult person. In fact, she routinely abused her son's wife. One might say that Monica had the patience of a saint. To ease the domestic pain, at some point she turned to drinking, a problem her son Augustine would also have to contend with later on. With the help of her faith, Monica eventually triumphed over her alcoholism and today those suffering from this problem invoke her in prayer.

St. Monica and her husband had three children: Augustine; a younger son, Navigius; and a daughter, Perpetua. While raising her children and attending to her irascible spouse's needs, Monica also found time to do good works for the poor and distribute alms in the commu-

With the help of her faith, Monica eventually triumphed over her alcoholism and today those suffering from this problem also invoke her in prayer.

nity. This charity only increased the wrath of Patricius, who thought she was throwing their money away. In time, the example of Monica's piety wore him down, and on his deathbed he became a Christian. Getting through to Augustine proved to be far more difficult. Every day and night Monica prayed for his conversion, but he seemed to be going farther and farther off the path of righteousness. Intellectually brilliant but lazy and egotistical, he fell in with adherents of the Manichaean religion, a pagan cult that preached the total incapacity of humans to do right. The Manichees preached that the world was a mistake, hence, we are unaccountable for our sins. When Monica heard Augustine spouting this nonsense at the dinner table, she threw him out of the house (and of course, being a mother, soon allowed him to return).

In desperation she sought the advice of a priest, who reassured her by saying, "It is not possible that the son of so many tears should perish"—perish spiritually, that is. Perpetua and Navigius had already become Christians, but it would take Augustine a lot longer—seventeen more years. During that time, his mother never gave up on him and actually followed him around the Mediterranean world while he pursued his dreams of academic glory and literary fame. Together they traveled all the way to Milan, in the northernmost part of Italy, where at last her faith and persistence were rewarded. There, she introduced her son to Ambrose, the bishop of Milan (and also a saint-to-be), who became Augustine's teacher. With Ambrose's spiritual guidance, and the help of a miraculous vision, Augustine repented, was converted, and went on to become one of the greatest teachers of Christianity in history.

Even though the ideal of the long-suffering mother is universal, St. Monica had a special appeal during the nineteenth century—a time when, perhaps, sons gave their mothers a particularly great deal to worry about.

Monica didn't have much time left to enjoy the fruits of her labors. She only lived another six months of perfect gratification after all those years of effort. On their return journey to North Africa, mother and son stopped at Ostia, a seaport near Rome, to wait for a ship home. Monica caught a fever in Ostia and died there at the age of fifty-four. The passages in Augustine's autobiography, *The Confessions*, in which he describes his mother's death, are among the most moving he ever wrote. Augustine relates that Navigius suggested that Monica be brought back to Africa for burial. But Monica said to Augustine, "Bury me here and don't let it be any trouble to you. The only thing I ask of you is that you remember me at the altar of the Lord wherever you may be."

Buried at Ostia, Monica's remains were forgotten until about two centuries later, when they were dug up and moved to a hidden crypt in the Church of St. Aureus in the town. In the fifteenth century, Pope Martin V had the relics transferred to Rome, and it is said that miracles occurred all along the route. Although there are no official records specifying a date, it is believed that St. Monica was canonized at this time. Later on, a French archbishop built a church in Rome specifically dedicated to St. Monica and buried her relics near the altar.

Even though the ideal of the long-suffering mother is universal, St. Monica had a special appeal during the nineteenth century—a time when, perhaps, sons gave their mothers a particularly great deal to worry about. In Paris in 1850, an Association of Christian Mothers was founded, with St. Monica as its patroness. The premise was that mothers whose sons (and husbands) had strayed from Christian life would band together and join their prayers into a mighty stream of maternal power. The idea took off, and within six years there were branches all over the world—in London, Dublin, Liverpool, Sydney, and Buenos Aires—drawing the wayward males back to the true path.

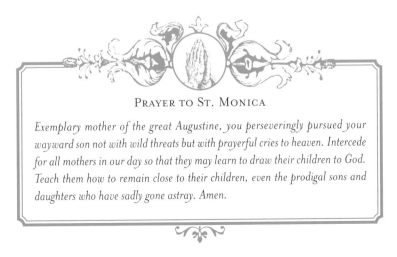

PRAYER TO ST. MONICA

Exemplary mother of the great Augustine, you perseveringly pursued your wayward son not with wild threats but with prayerful cries to heaven. Intercede for all mothers in our day so that they may learn to draw their children to God. Teach them how to remain close to their children, even the prodigal sons and daughters who have sadly gone astray. Amen.

St. Stephen

PATRON SAINT of
* HOME REPAIR * ODD JOBS AROUND THE HOUSE *
* STONEMASONS *

S T. STEPHEN has the unique distinction of being the first follower of Jesus to be killed for his faith. The Church calls St. Stephen the "protomartyr," and some pious writers have pointed out that he cast the first drops into what would eventually become a sea of bloodshed for the love of Christ.

Stephen was Jewish, but he was a little different from most of the other Jews who formed the early Church. His name—Stephanos, which means "crown"—is Greek, and he was most likely what we would call today an assimilated Jew, raised outside Israel and speaking Greek as his first language. As a preacher, he focused on spreading the word among other so-called Hellenized Jews like himself.

In those exciting first days of the Christian religion, everyone did a little of everything. Soon, however, the Apostles of the Church had to delegate. Stephen was made one of the first seven deacons, and was given the task of taking care of the physical needs of the poorest members of the new Christian community in Palestine.

Stephen attended to his assigned tasks, but he also kept teaching, and all who heard him agreed that he was filled with the Holy Spirit. He was universally known as a man of grace and wisdom. Among those who didn't hold this belief, however, were a few of his fellow Jews from the synagogues "of the Libertines, and of the Cyreneans, and of the Alexandrians, and of them that were of Cilicia and Asia," as it is said in the Book of Acts. They challenged Stephen to a debate. Not a good idea, considering that anyone who challenged an early Christian (fired up with the love of Christ and full of the eloquence of the Holy Spirit) to a debate usually came out the worse for wear. As it happened, it was Church 1, challengers 0, and the synagogue debaters were sore losers.

The challengers went straight to the police and had Stephen arrested and literally dragged before the Sanhedrin, the supreme council of the Jewish community, on charges that he had blasphemed the Jewish faith. They accused him of saying that Jesus would destroy the temple and change the laws and traditions that Moses had received on Mt. Sinai and handed down to the Israelites. That was untrue, and ironic considering that Stephen was a stonemason by trade and wasn't likely to be calling for the destruction of any building, let alone the sacred temple. In fact, Stephen is the patron saint of home repair, in homage to his former profession.

In any case, Stephen (ever the debater) made an impassioned defense to the court of his earlier remarks, explaining that Jesus' message was fully consistent with what the Old Testament said. He explained that God's mercies toward Israel were only being continued and expanded through Christianity, and that Jesus was the redeemer foretold by the Jewish prophets in centuries gone by. When he uttered the climactic words, "Behold, I saw the heavens opened, and the Son of Man standing at the right hand of God," there was nearly a riot in the courtroom. The Sanhedrin adjourned to deliberate the case, and when the elders reappeared, the sentence was death by stoning.

According to the custom, the convict was placed on a little hill and bound hand and foot, so that when the stoning began he would topple over, symbolizing his humiliation. When they got Stephen into this position, he called out, "Lord, lay not this sin to their charge." It was fitting that he did so, because one of the people in the crowd throwing stones at the martyr and pressing the heavy ones onto his body was none other than Saul, who would soon experience his own conversion and become St. Paul!

After Stephen died, his body was left unburied outdoors to be devoured by wild animals. A Jewish scholar, Rabban Gamaliel—not a Christian—took the corpse to his own country house in Caphargamala, about twenty miles outside Jerusalem, and entombed it there. For reasons that are unclear, the site's location was forgotten for several centuries. In A.D. 415, a local priest named Lucian had a dream in which Gamaliel appeared to him. Dressed in white and gold, the rabbi instructed him to go to Jerusalem, get the Bishop (who was named John), and then go with him to a certain spot and dig. In the tomb they would find the coffins of Gamaliel, his son Nicodemus (both of whom converted to Christianity), and St. Stephen. Lucian ignored the dream—one wonders why—but after it came to him

They found three coffins as promised, and when St. Stephen's was opened, an unexpectedly pleasant scent wafted out. A group of sick people was standing by, and seventy-three of them were cured of their illnesses on the spot.

a third time he bestirred himself to get Bishop John and carry out the task. They found three coffins as promised, and when St. Stephen's was opened, an unexpectedly pleasant scent wafted out. A group of sick people was standing by, and seventy-three of them were cured of their illnesses on the spot. Some of St. Stephen's relics were left in Caphargamala, but most were taken to Jerusalem and eventually made their way to Rome.

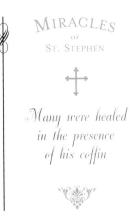

Many were healed in the presence of his coffin

Today, although his canonization date is unknown, St. Stephen is venerated as the patron saint of home repair, odd jobs around the house, stonemasons, and even interior construction—a sort of saintly Mr. Fixit. Perhaps a slightly odd fate for the first martyr of the Christian faith!

PRAYERS TO ST. STEPHEN

Oh glorious St. Stephen, first martyr for the Faith, filled with compassion for those who invoke you, with love for those who suffer, heavily laden with the weight of my troubles. I kneel at your feet and humbly beg you to take my present need(s) under your special protection [mention here]. Vouchsafe to recommend it to our Lord Jesus. Cease not to intercede for me until my request is granted. Amen.

Above all, obtain for me the grace to one day meet God face to face, and with you and Mary and all the angels and saints praise Him through all eternity. Oh most powerful St. Stephen, deacon and martyr, do not let me lose my soul, but obtain for me the grace of winning my way to heaven, forever and ever. Amen.

St. Teresa of Avila

PATRON SAINT *of*
* HEADACHE SUFFERERS *

ST. TERESA OF AVILA, or Teresa Sanchez Cepeda Davila y Ahumada was born in Avila, Spain, in 1515. She was raised by her parents in an atmosphere of such extreme piety that when Teresa was a little girl of seven, she announced to her family and friends that she wanted to go to the land of the Moors to be martyred. Her younger brother Rodrigo would join her, she said, and together they would ask the Muslims to cut their heads off. When her astounded parents asked her why, the embryonic saint replied, "So we can see God. Everyone knows you can't see Him until you die and go to Heaven." Teresa's adult life as a mystic would be devoted to disproving what "everyone knows."

Few little girls aspire to be missionaries and martyrs, so you would imagine that her path to sainthood would be a quick one. Not so. Teresa's adolescence was more typical. She was popular despite being superficial and disobedient, and got by without trying very hard at anything. Eventually, her strict father decided that she needed some discipline and sent her to the Carmelite convent at Avila—not an unusual step at the time. Many of the young women who lived in religious seclusion actually had no calling or aptitude for the religious life, and at first Teresa seemed to fit this mold. Despite her early promise, spiritually speaking, she was a late bloomer.

After a while spent in the convent, Teresa became seriously ill with malaria and went into convulsions. She was not expected to live, and when she finally woke up after days of unconsciousness and delirium, she was taken aback to hear that her grave had already been dug. Although she recovered, Teresa was never really healthy again and suffered one infirmity after another in her sixty-seven years of life. Perhaps the near-death experience inspired her to be more serious about her spiritual quest, or maybe she was just maturing, but Teresa resolved to change her ways. Her superiors at the convent were hopeful, but Teresa was still on the wrong path. Now she thought that she was so base and unworthy that she had no right to pray. Later, in her autobiography, Teresa described her ideas and behavior at the time as being like that of a baby deciding to turn away from its mother's breast. The only possible result could be death.

"God, deliver me from sullen saints."

—ST. TERESA OF AVILA

Finally, when she was forty-one years old, Teresa found her way to the Lord. A priest convinced her to pray and while she struggled with a restless mind, God eventually granted her visions and ecstasies. Her experiences grew so intense that she started levitating. This bizarre phenomenon irked Teresa because of the undue attention it attracted. She preferred to remain humbly inconspicuous. Instead, her contemporaries were talking about her, and not all the talk was kind. Many of Teresa's fellow Carmelites thought she was a freak or a fraud.

"Whenever we think of Christ we should recall the love that led him to bestow on us so many graces and favors, and also the great love God showed in giving us in Christ a pledge of his love; for love calls for love in return. Let us strive to keep this always before our eyes and to rouse ourselves to love him."

—St. Teresa of Avila

Friendship and good conversation had always been very important to Teresa, but now God was telling her they were distractions and that she must give them up. God told her, "I want you to only talk to angels now, not human beings." Eager to please, Teresa retreated into silence and contemplation. Some of her friends were worried and sent a priest to see her. He said her visions were false and that she must fight against them. If Jesus himself should appear to her, the priest instructed, Teresa should give him the finger (actually a Spanish gesture known as "the fig").

Teresa knew her experiences were real. She decided to break away from the convent and start her own order, one in which true contemplation wouldn't be discouraged. By founding the order of reformed Carmelites, also known as the Discalced (or barefoot) Carmelites, Teresa planted the seed of a new kind of spirituality that swept across Spain and eventually the rest of the world. Her close friend John (later canonized St. John of the Cross) worked with her to set up reformed Carmelite monasteries for men. Despite her poor health, Teresa traveled constantly, setting up convents and teaching Christian doctrine publicly. Her work was more the sort of thing a man would do in those days, and this provoked some harsh criticism. Even the Spanish Inquisition got on the case, but eventually found her blameless. Teresa put up with many hardships, but it was not her style to let challenges get her down. When a horse cart she was riding in on one of her missionary journeys got into an accident and she suffered a broken leg, she quipped, "Jesus, if this is the way you treat your friends, I can see why you have so few!" Despite her mystical, otherworldly pursuits, she always stressed cheerfulness and optimism. When a disciple asked Teresa how to meditate on Hell, she answered, simply, "Don't."

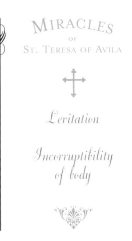

MIRACLES
OF
ST. TERESA OF AVILA

Levitation

Incorruptibility of body

Exhausted by her labors, Teresa died in 1582 and was canonized forty years later. Nine months after she was buried, her coffin collapsed and her body was exhumed. Miraculously, it was found to be undecayed and smelled sweetly perfumed. Her body was reburied and exhumed several more times. When it was last seen, in 1914, her body was reportedly still pristine, and the sweet scent was still present.

St. Teresa was canonized in 1622, and in 1970, Pope Paul VI declared her a Doctor of the Church, one of only two women in history to be so recognized.

Due to the physical pain and illnesses she had to endure, St. Teresa is the patron saint of headache sufferers.

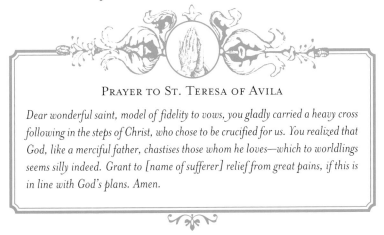

PRAYER TO ST. TERESA OF AVILA

Dear wonderful saint, model of fidelity to vows, you gladly carried a heavy cross following in the steps of Christ, who chose to be crucified for us. You realized that God, like a merciful father, chastises those whom he loves—which to worldlings seems silly indeed. Grant to [name of sufferer] relief from great pains, if this is in line with God's plans. Amen.

St. Thérèse of Lisieux

PATRON SAINT *of*
✳ MISSIONS ✳ FLORISTS ✳ THE SICK ✳

T. THÉRÈSE OF LISIEUX, known as the "Little Flower of Jesus," is a modern saint who has captured the hearts of millions worldwide. After her death in 1897, there was such a groundswell of support for her canonization that she was officially declared a saint in 1925. Yet this young woman, who only lived to be twenty-four, led an existence so uneventful that she was hardly noticed outside her tiny Carmelite convent. She went on no missions, never preached, wasn't martyred for the faith, and had no public role at all. What makes this saint so inspiring to so many people is her very ordinariness and simplicity. She showed that it isn't necessary to perform miraculous deeds to be holy and that the minutia of daily life can be sanctified.

Thérèse Martin was born in Normandy, in northern France, in 1873. Both her parents had had religious ambitions but failed to find vocations. For a while, still torn between worldly pleasures and a life devoted to God, they resisted consummating their marriage. Finally they gave in and had nine children, five of whom (all girls) survived childhood. The Martin sisters were close-knit and all of them eventually became nuns. The youngest was Thérèse.

As a little girl, Thérèse was headstrong and rather spoiled. Her mother died of breast cancer when Thérèse was only four years old, and her father indulged her a good deal after that. Her first brush with the religious life came at age nine, when she contracted a serious illness that nearly killed her. The entire family was standing around her bed, wondering whether she would pull through, when she looked over at a statue of the Virgin Mary and saw it smile at her. Instantly, Thérèse's sickness disappeared and she was filled with bliss. Soon she was praying all the time, sequestering herself in her room to talk to God and contemplate eternity.

As the baby of the family, Thérèse was coddled by her sisters. She was known for throwing tantrums and for bursting into tears at the slightest provocation—not very spiritually evolved things to do. That all changed on Christmas Eve when she was fourteen years old. As always, Thérèse left her shoes out to be filled with gifts, which is customary in France for little children, but not for adolescents Thérèse's age. Her father found it irritating that she was still so immature, and said that he hoped this would be the last year that she would leave her shoes out. Thérèse was about to cry, when all of a sudden a change came over her. She no longer had it in her to throw a tantrum, and realized that her father's feelings were more important than her own. Later, she called this moment her true conversion.

Following this episode, Thérèse was sure she had a vocation for the religious life, but she was considered too young to join the local Carmelite nunnery. Thérèse's father took her on a trip to Rome to distract her, but it had the opposite effect. While they were having an audience with Pope Leo XIII, Thérèse spoke out of turn and asked the Holy Father to grant her a special dispensation to become a Carmelite. He didn't reply, and she made such a fuss that they had to call security and escort her out of the room. Nonetheless, a high Catholic official who was present that day was impressed by Thérèse's gumption and recommended her to the nuns, who consented to accept her as a novice.

Life in the convent wasn't exactly what she had imagined it would be. She was lonely, and to make matters worse, the prayers that had been so soul-satisfying at home now seemed boring and empty. Thérèse decided not to let it get her down and made a practice of trying to be holy by making small, invisible sacrifices every day. She sacrificed in ways that nobody would notice, so that she would be denied the satisfaction of being recognized for what she had done. When her sister Pauline was elected prioress of the convent, Thérèse agreed to remain a permanent novice so that no one could suspect Pauline of showing her undue favor. Her humiliations were many. She called them the "little flowers" that she scattered for love's sake, having nothing bigger to offer.

Essentially, Thérèse's way was to remain a perpetual child. In her autobiography, *Story of a Soul*, which was written at the command of her superiors in the order, she wrote, "God would not make

> *"God would not make me wish for something impossible and so, in spite of my littleness, I can aim at being a saint. It is impossible for me to grow bigger, so I put up with myself as I am, with all my countless faults."*
>
> —St. Thérèse of Lisieux

me wish for something impossible and so, in spite of my littleness, I can aim at being a saint. It is impossible for me to grow bigger, so I put up with myself as I am, with all my countless faults. But I will look for some means of going to heaven by a little way which is very short and very straight, a little way that is quite new. We live in an age of inventions. We need no longer climb laboriously up flights of stairs; in well-to-do houses there are lifts. And I was determined to find a lift to carry me to Jesus, for I was far too small to climb the steep stairs of perfection.... It is your arms, Jesus, that are the lift to carry me to heaven. And so there is no need for me to grow up: I must stay little and become less and less."

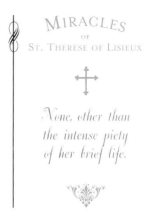

MIRACLES
OF
ST. THÉRÈSE OF LISIEUX

None, other than the intense piety of her brief life.

Thérèse died of tuberculosis at age twenty-four. She is the patron saint of missions (not because she ever went on one but because she supported them with letters of encouragement) and also of florists and those who are sick.

PRAYERS TO ST. THÉRÈSE OF LISIEUX

St. Thérèse, the Little Flower of Jesus, please pick a rose from the heavenly garden, and send it to me with a message of love. Amen.

If this favor is granted, I will love you more and more, and be better prepared to spend eternal happiness with you in heaven. Amen.

St. Thérèse, the Little Flower, pray for me. Amen.

St. Thomas Aquinas

PATRON SAINT of
* STUDENTS * SCHOLARS *
* ANYONE SEEKING KNOWLEDGE AND UNDERSTANDING *

ST. THOMAS' name derives from the town of Aquino, near Naples in southern Italy, where he was born in 1225. His parents were aristocrats, and they naturally expected that Thomas would follow in the family tradition, becoming adept at the manipulation of wealth and political clout. But from earliest childhood, the future saint stubbornly rejected his birthright; he was interested only in divinity.

At the age of seventeen, Thomas joined the Dominican order of friars. His parents were appalled, not only because their son had become a monk, but also because he had signed on with an order that was seen as lower class. The newly founded Dominicans preached in the streets, used the language of the ordinary people, and supported themselves by begging. When Thomas refused to take off his habit, his family—which seem to have been only a little less intimidating than the Sopranos—kidnapped him and locked him in their castle at Roccasecca. As if that weren't enough, his brothers organized a campaign of temptation against Thomas aimed at getting him to violate his vows. They sent a prostitute to his room to seduce him, but Thomas grabbed a hot coal and used it to chase the seductress from the room. The tearful begging and pleading of his mother and sisters didn't work any better than the brothers' tricks, and once they realized they couldn't "deprogram" him, Thomas' family let him return to his friars. He had been in confinement for two years.

Thomas' next step was college, first at the University of Naples and then at Cologne, Germany. For someone who would eventually be recognized by the Church as "Doctor Angelicus" the divine teacher, young Thomas didn't come across as an intellectual powerhouse. His fellow students called him "the dumb ox"—a reference both to his inarticulate nature and his hefty body mass. Even so, one of his professors, Albertus Magnus—a great doctor of the Church and a future saint, although reputed by some to be a magician and alchemist—saw embryonic genius waiting to emerge. "I tell you," he reprimanded the doubters, "that one day this ox will bellow so loud that it will

> *"Sorrow can be alleviated by good sleep, a bath, and a glass of wine."*
>
> — ST. THOMAS

resound throughout the entire world." Indeed, Thomas' two massive works of religious philosophy, the *Summa Theologica* and the *Summa Contra Gentiles*, continue to guide the thinking of devout Catholics to this day.

His studies completed, Thomas became a teacher himself, mainly in Paris and Rome. While in the French capital, he became friendly with the saintly King Louis, advising him on spiritual matters and often dining at royal banquets. On one famous occasion at a state dinner, Thomas behaved a little strangely. While the society people chattered away and the courtiers talked politics, Thomas seemed to be daydreaming. All of a sudden, he brought his fist crashing down on the table, causing plates and glasses to jump. "That settles the Manichees!" he declared, and summoned his secretary to take down an argument against a heretical sect for the book he was working on. His tablemates said, "Don't you realize you're at dinner with the king? Show some respect." Thomas, suddenly abashed, answered that he had been so deep in thought that he imagined he was alone in his cell. The king told him not to worry and sent his own scribe to take down Thomas' insight.

> *"Good can exist without evil, whereas evil cannot exist without good."*
>
> — St. Thomas

Thomas' life was one of traveling, preaching, teaching, and writing. Although a great intellectual, he was always humble and refused many high positions, even when Pope Clement IV offered to make him an archbishop. Thomas also realized that reason should always take second place to love and faith. Toward the end of his life, he had a vision while praying in church and henceforth refused to write anything more, saying, "Such secrets have been revealed to me that all I have written now seems like so much straw."

> *"Friendship is the source of the greatest pleasures, and without friends even the most agreeable pursuits become tedious."*
>
> — St. Thomas

His greatest work, the *Summa Theologica*, was left unfinished. In 1274, Pope Gregory X summoned him to a Church council at

Lyons, France. Despite illness, Thomas obediently set out to walk there from Rome. Not long into the journey, Thomas fell over on the road and was taken to the Cistercian monastery at Fossa Nuova, where he died at the age of forty-nine. He was canonized on July 18th, 1328. The priest who heard his last confession said later that it was as simple and guileless as that of a five-year-old child. Thomas's only real sin was overeating.

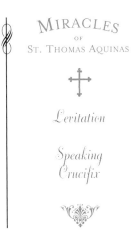

While Thomas was quiet and unobtrusive, miracles occasionally happened around him. On one occasion, some of his students entered his room unannounced and found him levitating. A crucifix on the wall suddenly started speaking, saying, "You have written well of me, Thomas. What reward would you like?" He answered, "Nothing other than thyself, Lord."

St. Thomas is the patron saint of college students, scholars, and anyone seeking knowledge and understanding.

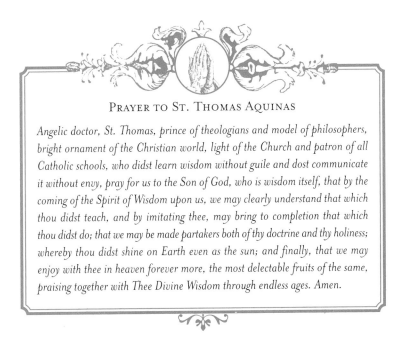

PRAYER TO ST. THOMAS AQUINAS

Angelic doctor, St. Thomas, prince of theologians and model of philosophers, bright ornament of the Christian world, light of the Church and patron of all Catholic schools, who didst learn wisdom without guile and dost communicate it without envy, pray for us to the Son of God, who is wisdom itself, that by the coming of the Spirit of Wisdom upon us, we may clearly understand that which thou didst teach, and by imitating thee, may bring to completion that which thou didst do; that we may be made partakers both of thy doctrine and thy holiness; whereby thou didst shine on Earth even as the sun; and finally, that we may enjoy with thee in heaven forever more, the most delectable fruits of the same, praising together with Thee Divine Wisdom through endless ages. Amen.

St. Valentine

PATRON SAINT *of*
* LOVE * YOUNG PEOPLE *

ST. VALENTINE (or Valentinus), the patron saint of love and young people, was no dewy-eyed romantic but a priest in ancient Rome who was martyred for his faith. In the third century A.D., under the reign of the brutal Emperor Claudius the Goth, Roman Christians had to live in secret. In those dark days, the faithful were reduced to skulking about in underground passages called catacombs in an attempt to elude persecutors and practice their religion in peace.

Thanks to his devout Christian beliefs, Valentine was eventually hauled up before a tribunal where he was charged with propagating his religion and helping Christians. Aiding Christians in any way was considered a crime, and Valentine was quite forthcoming with his guilt. One of the many ways in which he helped them was to perform marriages, and that is the primary reason why St. Valentine is prayed to for help in finding everlasting, perfect love.

The emperor himself interrogated Valentine, asking him why he rejected the Roman way and sided with the enemies of the empire. The future saint responded that he was no traitor, but simply believed in a higher power and a higher love. He told Claudius that if he accepted Jesus Christ and worshipped the one true God, the ruler would find contentment. One of the judges, tiring of Valentine's eloquence, brusquely interrupted and asked the priest what he thought of the pagan deities Jupiter and Mercury. "That they were miserable, and spent their whole lives in debauchery and crime!" shot back the martyr-to-be.

The judges were on the verge of convicting Valentine, but the emperor's curiosity was piqued and he allowed the prisoner to continue. The priest urged Claudius to repent for all the Christians he had killed and told him that if he were to become a Christian himself, far from betraying Rome, he would ensure her lasting military victory and economic prosperity. This kind of talk appealed to the ruler; he began to be swayed and was pretty close to converting when his resolve inexplicably crumbled and he handed Valentine over to another court.

The new judge was called Asterius. He had a daughter who had been blinded by an illness two years earlier, and he challenged Valentine to demonstrate the truth of his faith by restoring her sight. If God was the light of the world, it should be no problem for Him to bring the light back to the girl's eyes, Asterius contended. Valentine—in this case willing to cast pearls before swine—worked the miracle and cured her. Asterius was overwhelmed by this evidence of the power of faith and became a Christian right away, as did his daughter and the rest of his family. Things were looking up for Valentine, but the emperor, now fully reinvested in his paganism, was outraged to hear what had happened and condemned Valentine to summary execution.

It is said that while waiting in his cell to be martyred, St. Valentine wrote a farewell note to Asterius's daughter and signed it, "From your Valentine."

In 268, together with several other Christians, Valentine was tortured, beaten with clubs, stoned, and finally beheaded. His body was buried on the Flaminian Way in Rome, in a tomb which has since been unearthed by modern archaeologists. It is said that while waiting in his cell to be martyred, Valentine wrote a farewell note to Asterius' daughter and signed it, "From your Valentine." Lovers have been using that memorable phrase ever since.

Although Valentine's canonization date is no longer known, Pope Gelasius officially recognized February 14 as St. Valentine's Day in 496. It is telling that birds choose their mates around this time, and in medieval poetry, the ritual of lovers courting each other on Valentine's Day was compared to the mating rituals of birds. Representations of St. Valentine usually depict him surrounded by birds and roses.

Still, it seems rather a long journey from martyr to matchmaker. Not until the late Middle Ages—around the fifteenth century—did the sending of valentines become customary. This was the age of the troubadours, who composed odes in celebration of courtly love. The oldest surviving valentine was written by Charles, Duke of Orleans, a French soldier who was captured by the English at the battle of Agincourt in 1415. He wrote the tender greeting from the Tower of London to his wife back home, and somehow it has been preserved in the British Library. Perhaps it was never sent. King Henry V of England, who personally led his troops to victory in that same battle, also wrote a valentine, or rather, he had one of his court writers, John Lydgate, ghostwrite it for him. The recipient was no less a personage than his wife Catherine of Valois, daughter of Charles VI of France.

Though these valentines were basically secular and worldly—if not actually carnal in intent—it was still a religious age, and interest in matters of the heart went hand in hand with Christian veneration. St. Valentine was extremely popular in both England and France in those days. By the eighteenth century, however, Valentine's Day had pretty much lost its devout overtones. English people of all classes were sending valentines, and by the middle of the nineteenth century, the loving messages were being mass-produced, much as they are today. Even in the twenty-first century, however, February 14 can be a day to reflect on the connection between human and divine love.

The relics of St. Valentine survive to this day, preserved in the Whitefriar Street Church in Dublin, Ireland. They stayed in Rome until 1835, when Pope Gregory XVI heard an Irish priest called John Spratt preaching in the Eternal City and was impressed by what he heard. As a token of appreciation, the Holy Father gave the Irishman St. Valentine's earthly remains. They are displayed to the public every Valentine's Day, protected by a casket colored gold and black—not red and pink.

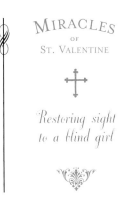

MIRACLES
OF
ST. VALENTINE

Restoring sight to a blind girl

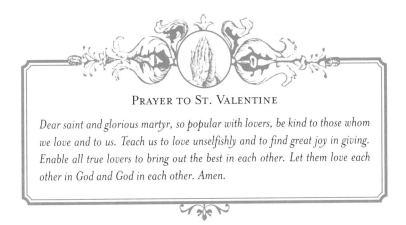

PRAYER TO ST. VALENTINE

Dear saint and glorious martyr, so popular with lovers, be kind to those whom we love and to us. Teach us to love unselfishly and to find great joy in giving. Enable all true lovers to bring out the best in each other. Let them love each other in God and God in each other. Amen.

St. Zita of Lucca

PATRON SAINT of
MAIDS ✳ DOMESTICS ✳ HOUSEWORK ✳
THOSE WHO ARE MOCKED FOR THEIR PIETY

S̶T. ZITA OF LUCCA was born in 1218 to a poor family in the Tuscan village of Monte Sagrati. Zita was raised in an atmosphere of such intense piety that all her mother had to do to make sure she did the right thing was to ask gently, "Is this pleasing to God, or not?" Zita never let anything but God's will guide her.

The family was known for its holiness—her uncle Graziano was a hermit whom the locals venerated as a saint, and her older sister joined a Cistercian abbey as a nun. As for Zita, she was destined not for a famous religious community but for the deeper humility of domestic service. She spent her entire life as a maid and achieved such holiness through her work that she became the patron saint of housekeepers, domestic servants, and housework.

At the age of twelve, Zita went to work as a maid in the nearby city of Lucca for the wealthy Fatinelli family, who were in the weaving business. She distinguished herself immediately by her devotion to duty and her quiet seriousness. Zita believed that work is a penance placed upon mankind for its sins and that cheerfully bearing that burden is the path to spiritual growth and redemption. She saw obedience to her employers as a reflection of obedience to God.

In addition to her other pious acts, Zita fasted on bread and water, sometimes for an entire year, and slept in the attic on the bare floorboards without benefit of mattress, pillow, or blanket.

One would think that with an attitude like that, Zita would have been considered the ideal employee. But alas, that was not the case. For one thing, Mr. Fatinelli was what would today be called a boss from hell, and repeatedly exploded in displays of ill temper. Even more importantly, Zita's conspicuous piety aroused resentment throughout the Fatinelli family and among her fellow workers. She made it her habit to get up hours before everyone else so she could attend Mass at the Church of St. Frigidian next door, perform her private meditations and prayers, and still have time to get breakfast ready for the family and attend to her domestic chores. In addition to her other pious acts, Zita fasted on bread and water, sometimes for an entire year, and slept in the attic on the bare floorboards without benefit of mattress, pillow, or blanket. She also developed the ability to say prayers while going about her business, no matter what she was doing, and if any other servant threatened to be a bad influence in the household, she would denounce him or her to the Fatinellis. For instance, when a male servant spoke immodestly, Zita got him fired. Perhaps that was part of why she was resented, although she was also known for defending any servant whose small mistakes aroused the wrath of Mr. Fatinelli. Be that as it may, the word got out in the household that Zita was "holier than thou." Of course, in this case, it was literally true!

In time, she won over the Fatinellis, who came to realize they had a future saint in their midst. Miraculous happenings may have had something to do with it. On one occasion, Zita was so absorbed in her prayers at church that she forgot to get back to the kitchen in time to bake the bread. She came out of her trance with a start and ran frantically back to the house, where she found the bread already baked. Far too humble to think that she could be favored with an overt manifestation of divine grace, Zita

The bread had been baked by angels while Zita was praying.

assumed that one of the other servants or even the master and mistress of the house must have done the baking for her. She ran to thank them and apologize for her dereliction, but they had no idea what she was talking about. The bread had been baked by angels while Zita was praying.

Once they were won over, the Fatinellis remained loyal to her and rewarded Zita by making her the head of the domestic staff. They were no longer annoyed that their maid helped the poor by distributing some of her wages and even household funds as alms. Her piety, formerly mocked, was now admired. In her humility, she had never wanted recognition or a position of power. Now that she was in charge of the house, though, she took her duties to heart, practicing the strictest economy and generally running a tight ship. Now that she had the ability to delegate some tasks, she was able to spend more time helping the poor and sick outside the house. Her selfless acts made her famous throughout Lucca—so famous, in fact, that after her death, the city was often referred to as "Santa Zita."

In all, Zita spent forty-eight years in service and died in harness in 1278, at the age of sixty. When she died, a star suddenly appeared in the sky. To the onlookers below, it seemed to hang right above the attic where she had her bedroom. In 1580, her body was exhumed and found to be in a state of incorruptibility. Zita, the handmaid of the Lord, was canonized in 1696.

To this day, St. Zita's body is kept on display in the Church of St. Frigidian, right next to the former Fatinelli house. St. Zita's face and hands are visible, uncovered, through a plate of glass.

In addition to being the patron saint of housekeepers and servants, St. Zita is the patron of those who are mocked for their piety.

MIRACLES
OF
ST. ZITA OF LUCCA

Neglected bread found baked

Star in sky signaling her death

Incorruptibility of body

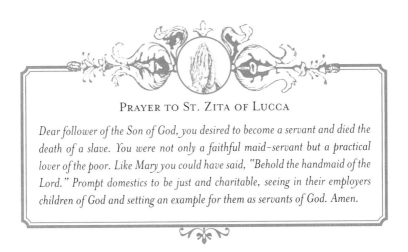

PRAYER TO ST. ZITA OF LUCCA

Dear follower of the Son of God, you desired to become a servant and died the death of a slave. You were not only a faithful maid-servant but a practical lover of the poor. Like Mary you could have said, "Behold the handmaid of the Lord." Prompt domestics to be just and charitable, seeing in their employers children of God and setting an example for them as servants of God. Amen.

Calendar of Feast Days

N THE CALENDAR OF THE CATHOLIC CHURCH, every saint has a special day on which his or her feast—or festival—is celebrated. Usually the date is the one on which the saint died or was martyred. Of course, since there are far more than 365 saints, each day could see a feast in honor of any one of several saints. On each feast day, special ceremonies are carried out around the world in communities that venerate the particular saint being celebrated. Such veneration usually originates from a personal connection the saint had in life with that geographic area. It is also customary for many Catholics to name a child after one of the saints whose feast day coincides with the child's birthday. Finally, a saint's feast day provides us with an opportunity to recall that saint's life and death and to make a special prayer to him or her of honor and remembrance. The following is a list of the feast days and areas of expertise in the domestic sphere for each of the saints illuminated in this book.

ST. AGATHA * *breast cancer, foundry workers, protection against fire, mountain guides*
February 5

ST. ANTHONY OF PADUA * *finding lost objects*
June 13

ST. AUGUSTINE * *brewers*
August 28

ST. BARBARA * *good marriage, artillerymen, protection from lightning*
December 4

ST. CLARE OF ASSISI * *television, television writers*
August 11

ST. DYMPHNA * *protection from anxiety, mental illness*
May 15

ST. FRANCIS OF ASSISI * *animals, ecology, merchants*
October 4

ST. FRANCIS DE SALES * *journalists, writers*
January 24

ST. GERARD MAJELLA * *expectant mothers*
October 16

ST. JOSEPH * *house hunting, getting a good price for one's house*
March 19

ST. JUDE * *lost or desperate causes*
October 28

ST. LAWRENCE * *cooks, chefs, protection against kitchen accidents*
August 10

ST. MARTIN DE PORRES * *barbers, hairstylists, the lovelorn*
November 3

ST. MONICA * *mothers, relationship advice, alcoholics, those who are abused*
August 27

ST. STEPHEN * *home repair, odd jobs around the house, stonemasons*
December 26

ST. TERESA OF AVILA * *headache sufferers*
October 15

ST. THÉRÈSE OF LISIEUX * *missions, florists, the sick*
October 1

ST. THOMAS AQUINAS * *students, scholars, anyone seeking knowledge and understanding*
January 28

ST. VALENTINE * *love, young people*
May 2

ST. ZITA OF LUCCA * *maids, domestics, housework, those who are mocked for their piety*
April 27

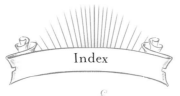

Index

Resources

THE RESOURCES USED TO CREATE THIS BOOK ARE:

Catholic Online: Saints & Angels
http://www.catholic.org/saints/

Magnificat Calendar of the Saints
http://www.magnificat.ca/cal/engl/liste-sts.htm

Catholic Encyclopedia Online
http://www.newadvent.org/cathen/index

Catholic Forum Saints Index
http://www.catholic-forum.com/saints/indexsnt.htm

Butler, Alban. *The Lives of the Fathers, Martyrs, and Other Principal Saints, 5 vols.* Catholic Press, 1956.

Calamari, Barbara and Sandra di Pasqua. *The Novena Book: The Power of Prayer.* Penguin, 1999.

Luce, Clare Boothe ed. *Saints for Now.* Ignatius Press, 1993.

The Holy Bible, New Testament.